Jacob B Eaton,

70

NATURE STUDY TEXTBOOK
FOR
SIXTH GRADE

"The woods are just behind our house,
  And every afternoon at four
I go to pick the lovely flowers
  That grow right up beside the door."

NATURE STUDY

By JOHN BRADFORD CRAIG

NATURE STUDY

PITTSBURGH TEACHERS' TRAINING SCHOOL

PITTSBURGH, PENNSYLVANIA

BOOK IV

ILLUSTRATED

McINDOO PUBLISHING COMPANY

KANSAS CITY, MISSOURI

1921

CONTENTS

"Jack-in-the-pulpit
Preaches today
Under the green trees,
Just over the way."

PREFACE

During the sixth, seventh, and eighth years of school life, pupils cease to be entirely satisfied with interesting and instructive stories or even with interesting observation. There is a constructive desire to react to the stimuli presented and to produce something.

Education that does not find its interpretation in a utility of the broadest meaning is out of tune with modern civilization.

The time has gone, if it ever existed, when the aristocracy of any state could be explained by the formulae of leisure and wealth. The real aristocracy of the future civilization must have at its center the spirit of effort and service. In no way may pupils develop this spirit to a better advantage than by a careful experimental knowledge of nature and her laws of production as they relate to health and happiness.

Many mature people do not know how potatoes grow nor why apples drop from the trees when they have just begun to develop. Their children should know.

A sane feeling of importance and worth comes to the pupil when he knows he has produced something and is intelligent concerning the laws which govern the process of its production.

There is no greater anchor to happiness and independence than the knowledge and the ability to produce food in an efficient manner. There is no ballast more effective in the stability of any state than an efficient army of food producers. In order that such an army may be created the fundamental elements must be learned by all pupils in the public schools.

This text is meant to give, in an elementary way, a few of the essential elements of natural science in its relation to plant growth.

In order that the content of this text may be used most effectively, the work here outlined must not be done for the pupil but must be done by the pupil under proper supervision and instruction.

J. B. C.

INTRODUCTORY STORY

During the early days of March, 1918, a teacher in one of the schools of a large American city told her pupils about the great war that was then in progress in Europe. She explained why men from America were being sent across the ocean to fight. She told how homes were being burned, how women and little children were being killed and that brave American soldiers were being sent to stop this great evil. She also said that all of the men, women, boys, and girls in America must help these soldiers if they were to succeed. Two things, she said, boys and girls could do that would help just as much as the work the soldiers were doing. The first of these, she said, was to plant a garden so that there might be a large supply of food for the soldiers and also sufficient for those at home. The second thing was to save money and lend it to the government by buying thrift stamps so that the government might have sufficient money to pay the expenses of the army in Europe. This, she said, was very important because America was using several million men in the army and navy, and the allied countries also had a large number of soldiers. These men were not able to produce food, as many of them had been doing before they became soldiers.

These men not only needed to be fed but other people must do the planting and produce the food which these soldiers had been producing before the war.

In this school were two boys, John and Jim, who were neighbors. John was twelve years of age and Jim was ten. Their parents were poor and were not able to live in large and beautiful houses and have large lawns and gardens as many people had. Jim's brother had gone to the great war. John's father was dead and he had no brothers or sisters. Although John was a selfish boy he tried to feel patriotic because he now knew why Jim's brother had gone to help the American soldiers fight the men who had destroyed so many homes and left so many orphans in Europe.

After listening to what the teacher said about the great School Garden Army that was about to be organized in their city, each of these boys began to feel enthusiastic about becoming soldiers in this army. After the teacher had finished and the regular school work was continued, John began to consider the work that would be necessary to operate a garden and the more he thought about the work the less patriotic he became and the less anxious to join such an army.

Jim waited outside of the building that evening until John's room was dismissed. Jim had never had a garden and he knew nothing about one. He had visions of producing loads of tomatoes, potatoes, onions, beans, peas, and a lot of other things which the teacher had mentioned but which he could not remember.

As soon as John was out of school these two boys started home together. They were together most of their time when out of school.

A VEGETABLE GARDEN AND BOY
This boy is holding a bean pod in his hands

"Did your teacher say anything today about gardens and the great School Garden Army that they are going to start in all of the schools?" said Jim. "Yes," replied John, in a very indifferent tone of voice. "She gave us a long speech about the war, the army, the people in Europe, gardens, food, and I don't remember what all she did say." "Aren't you going to join the School Garden Army then?" exclaimed Jim in surprise. "No!" replied John, "how could I plant a garden? I have no place for a garden and I don't know how to make one if I did have a place." "I didn't think about the place," said Jim in a somewhat discouraged tone of voice. "But," argued Jim, "we can find a place somewhere." "Well, suppose you did have a place, you haven't any seed and you haven't any tools to work with." "What do you want tools for?" Jim asked. "Tools!" exclaimed John, "a garden won't grow by just watching it. You've got to work it and hoe it. Oh! I'll tell you it's a lot of work to make a garden." "The teacher told us she would explain all about how the work was done," persisted Jim. "Well, suppose she did, she won't do any of the work for you, you can depend on that," argued John in defense of the position he had taken. "Suppose it is a lot of work to do all the teacher said and suppose it is a lot more work to do what she said she was going to tell us, it's a lot of work to fight over in Europe too, and somebody must do it, and if we don't do part of it, that will just leave more for the others to do. Somebody must do some work to get enough food to feed my brother and all of the other soldiers until they come home." "The government will feed the soldiers," said John, "the government always takes good care of its soldiers." "I know it does," replied Jim sharply, "but where is it going to get the food to give them?" "Why, from the farmer, of course," retorted John. "It's the farmer's business to raise potatoes and beans and whatever is necessary for people to eat." "Where does your mother get the potatoes you eat at home?" questioned Jim with a persistence which seemed beyond his years. "From the grocery store," said John, "where do you suppose she gets them, from the jewelry store?" "No, I didn't suppose she got them at the jewelry store, but don't you know that the government must get them from the grocer or from the farmer, and if the government needs all the farmer has or that the grocer can get, then your mother can't get any and you must do without? That means that somebody must go hungry. Miss Bonzo told us today that there were many people in Europe now who were starving." "Well!" said John, being almost convinced by Jim's argument, "if Miss Bonzo furnishes me with a place for a garden, buys the seed, furnishes the tools, and tells me what to do, I'll plant a garden."

"It's nothing to Miss Bonzo," said Jim, "whether you plant a garden or not. She's only doing the best she can to back up the government, my brother, and the other soldiers. You're a slacker, you are!" and little patriotic Jim's lip was trembling with anger. "I'm going to find a place for a garden myself and I'm going to use some of the money that I have saved for a bicycle to buy tools and seed and I'm going to be a real soldier in the School Garden Army. Nobody will ever call me a slacker. You know slackers can't salute the flag like we did this morning in school."

They separated. One going to his home angry but proud of himself, proud of his brother, and proud of his country, the kind of pride that makes men out of boys, and the kind of pride that has always made our flag respected by every nation on the face of the earth. The other went to his home but not so happy as he generally was. He knew Jim's brother was no slacker and he didn't feel that he would be either if he were old enough to go to war and have a gun to carry. He didn't feel that anyone should be called a slacker unless he refused to do his part as a soldier in the real army.

After supper John did what work he had to do but everything seemed to go wrong. John didn't know that everything always goes wrong when men or women, boys or girls, do things which make them ashamed to stand before a glass and respect what they see.

John's mother had taught him to say his prayers at her knee before he went to his bed for the night.

"Don't you feel well?" said his mother, when he had finished and was about to kiss her goodnight. "You don't look well." "Oh yes," said John, "I feel all right," and started for his room.

When he had reached the door he turned as though he had forgotten something. "Mother, what is a slacker?" he asked. "Why, my son, a slacker is anyone who does not want to help his country, his city, his home, or himself when help is needed. He does not want to do his full duty and would rather other people would do his work for him. A slacker, my son, is a selfish person who wants to avoid the hard jobs and tries to get on as easy in the world as he can. He will even pretend he is ill when the country needs soldiers, just as some dishonest boys sometimes pretend they are ill and unable to do their share of work either at home or in school. They are slackers just the same as the soldier who runs away from the battle."

With his mother's words running back and forth through his mind he finally fell asleep.

During the night he had an awful dream. In his dream he was taken up in the air in a large machine of some kind. He had never seen anything like it before. It was with great difficulty that he held on to the machine for a strong wind was blowing. John did not mind the wind so much as he did the little imp-like person who drove the machine and who seemed to be humming a tune to himself as he drove through the air. John could not catch any of the words very well but he thought he heard the word slacker two or three times. Even the wind, as it tore through the machine, seemed to stop long enough to whisper slacker in his ear as it rushed by.

After a wonderful ride through the clouds the

machine seemed to be dropping and sliding down toward the ground just as John had often seen leaves fall from the trees in the late summer. Even this feeling of falling to the ground would not have frightened John so much, although it was bad enough, if it had not been for this imp who sat facing him as he drove the machine and, with a sneer on his face, seemed to be saying "slacker, slacker, slacker," in a hissing sound through his teeth.

At last with a sudden thump, which almost threw John out of the machine, they struck the ground. The little imp seemed to be beside him at once and very roughly took hold of John's arm and hustled him through the woods to what seemed to John, in the dim starlight which was shining through the trees, to be an old building of some kind. It looked something like the hunters' cabins he had read about in story books.

By this time John was trembling with fear. The wind was still blowing and it whipped the tall, damp, and ragged weeds against his face. Surely the man who lives in such a place is a slacker, thought John. But he was too much frightened to think about anything but himself and this awful imp. John wondered if he would ever get back home and whether or not he would ever see Jim again. He wondered what this imp was planning to do with him at this old house, and if he were to be shut up here. Nothing looked familiar to John. The trees around seemed taller than any he had ever seen. Even the high hill across the ravine below this old house, which he could just make out in the darkness, seemed strange. John wished he were at home. He would be glad to plant gardens. He knew he could earn money for seed and tools. He would be glad to do all of these things and more. He would do anything if he could just get away from this awful imp and get back home.

John wondered if this was a punishment for him because he did not want to join the School Garden Army. Was he a slacker? Are all people who are slackers punished? Many such thoughts flashed through John's mind in the very few minutes needed to get to this old house which John thought might be his prison.

Suddenly they reached the old cabin and the imp opened the door which squeaked on its rusty hinges. With what seemed to John the strength of a giant, the imp picked him up and threw him inside. It was dark, very dark, inside and John could not see anything. He fell to the floor which broke through with his weight and down, down, down he went. Was this a well he had stepped into or rather had been thrown into? Wells have bottoms but this one did not seem to have any. He could hear water running but it seemed a great way off. He reached out and clutched at the sides. At last he grasped what seemed to him the limb of a tree. With desperate effort he held on. Where was he? He rubbed his eyes with his free hand and looked around. It was daylight. He was holding fast to the post of his own bed! The birds were singing outside and the sun was beginning to shine in through the windows just as it had always done. He was glad that he was at home and could go back to school.

The teacher appointed one Captain, two Lieutenants, and four Corporals in each room. The Captain was the superior officer. Under him were the Lieutenants and under the Lieutenants were the Corporals. Under most of the Corporals were seven pupils. This group of seven together with the Corporal made up a squad or a garden unit. There were two squads, or garden units, under each Lieutenant. John was made a Corporal.

After each Captain received his commission

from the principal of the school and it was endorsed by the teacher, he called his Lieutenants together and gave them the following orders:

1st. Each Lieutenant must make certain that the Corporals under his command provide a garden site for each student.

2d. All rubbish such as tin cans, weeds, and brush must be removed from these garden sites.

3d. Each Lieutenant must report the work completed within one week.

Before school was dismissed the teachers announced that the Lieutenants had issued an order for a meeting of all Corporals and privates immediately after school.

At this meeting it was found that all of the pupils but two in John's squad already had places for gardens. John's superior officer, Lieutenant Brown, detailed John and two of the privates, Bill Rogers and Sam Hart, both of whom were in John's squad, to secure sites for the two pupils who did not have gardens. This was to be done by nine o'clock on the following morning.

After the meeting was over, John, in company with Bill and Sam, started to look for a site.

"We don't have to do this work, do we?" said Bill. To this John replied sharply, "You're under orders, Bill, and neither the government nor I will tolerate slackers on this job." John felt the responsibilities of his office very keenly. "If you are going to be a slacker and a quitter you will have to get into some other squad. This squad is under my charge and we have orders to get two garden sites, and two garden sites we're going to get."

After they had walked two or three squares talking over where they might find a vacant lot, Sam suggested that they call on old Mr. Nesbit who lived just around the corner in a large brick house. "He has three large vacant lots and there never was anything growing on them but weeds," said Sam. "He wouldn't give you anything," interrupted Bill. "He won't allow the boys to sled ride down the hill past his house any longer than he can get ashes scattered on the track." "Suppose we ask him," said John. "He can't any more than turn us down," and the three boys hurried around the corner to where Mr. Nesbit lived. They found him at home. Very politely John told him of the plan they had arranged at school for learning how to cultivate gardens. John told him also that while the great war lasted and the government needed extra food, they intended to make a special effort in order that as much food as possible might be produced. When he had finished, Mr. Nesbit seemed very much interested. "What can I do to help you, my son?" asked he. "You have two or three slacker lots over on Second street that we want to use if you will give us permission to clean them off and turn them into gardens," said John in a very businesslike tone of voice. "I should be very happy to have you use my lots in this way," replied the old gentleman, "if I felt you would not grow tired of your job and quit when the gardens had just started to grow." The word *quit* was the word which John had learned in recent days to hate. He had heard of deserters in the government's army quitting and he had heard of men refusing to help the Red Cross, and to all of these people he had affixed the word *quitter*. "Mr. Nesbit," said John with the dignity of an army officer, "the squad that wants to use your lots is under my command. I am the Corporal of the squad and the fellow that turns out to be a slacker and a quitter will have to reckon with me." "That's the spirit, boys. That's the spirit I like to see in soldiers" said Mr. Nesbit. "You may use my lots and if you have any boy in your squad who does not have money to buy tools or seed, I will get them for him and he can pay me back in vegetables when they grow." John thanked him and the boys left with the opinion that Mr. Nesbit was in reality their friend and a gentleman.

Before the following Monday morning, each Corporal saw to it that each boy in his squad had all of the rubbish removed from his garden and that it was in good condition for plowing. The rubbish that would burn was destroyed in this way, and what would not burn was hauled away.

On this Monday morning the Captain of each room announced that each Monday evening and on wet evenings when no work could be done in the gardens, and sometimes during school hours, the teacher or principal would give instruction in gardening.

During the day the principal went to each room and announced that an exhibition of what the pupils had grown in their gardens would be given in the late summer or fall. At this exhibition medals of honor would be given for efficient work and a silk banner to the squad having the best exhibition of garden products.

During the physical exercise period, John called

EXHIBIT OF GARDEN CLUB WORK OF BOYS AND GIRLS, GRAND RAPIDS, MICHIGAN

AN EXHIBIT OF WHAT ONE BOY DID

He made $143.50 off of 5,000 square feet of muck soil, Grand Rapids, Michigan

Bill aside from the other pupils and said, "Do you know Jim Stuart, the man who has a stable down on Corporation street and College avenue where he keeps his horses?" "Yes, I know him well; I was on his wagon last Saturday," replied Bill. "Well, now, listen," said John, "our squad is about to get that silk banner which Mr. McCollough announced in the rooms today." "Why, we haven't even planted our gardens," broke in Bill before John had finished. "Well, wait until I get through; I haven't told you how we are about to get this banner. You know you can't grow much of a garden in this part of the country without fertilizer and the best kind of fertilizer is stable manure." "Why can't you grow a garden without fertilizer?" said Bill. "Well, you can't and I know you can't because I've been out at my grandfather's farm enough to know that," said John with an attitude of authority. "What I want you to do is this, I want you to go and see Jim Stuart just as quickly as your feet can get you to him after school this evening. Tell him you are a member of the School Garden Army, Grant Battalion, Company C, and that you have orders to ask him for all of his stable manure to be used on the gardens of your squad. Also explain to him why we are planting gardens and he may not charge you so much. Find out what his bill will be and tell him we will expect it sent to gardens that I shall indicate, and sent C. O. D. It is the early bird that catches the worm, you know. I don't want you to loaf any until you have secured his entire stock for the next two months. The other fellows haven't begun to think about fertilizer yet and many of them don't know that we have to use it, and lots of it, on the garden if we are going to have a good garden. Now I am depending on you to get that manure from Mr. Stuart and you must do it this evening. You never get anywhere if you put things off. There isn't any squad that's going to win over our squad if I can help it." Just then the bell rang and the boys went back to their classrooms.

Bill, however, kept in mind his orders. After school the teacher gave the first lesson in gardening, and as soon as Bill could get away, he lost no time until he had secured all of the manure in Mr. Stuart's stable and had obtained a promise of the next two month's supply. He was so polite and manly in the way he asked for it and made it so plain that he wanted it for the school garden that Mr. Stuart promised it to him without charge

if the boys would load it on his wagon when he
found time to haul it.

With a great deal of satisfaction, Bill reported to Corporal John his success.

* * * * * * *

The following lessons are those given by the
teachers to the pupils. The work of each pupil in
his garden was inspected by the Corporal of the
squad once each week.

Each Lieutenant received from the Corporals
under him a report, oral or written, once each
week. These reports contained the kind and amount
of work done, the kind, amount, and cost of
manure, and seed used, and the difficulties which
the pupil met in his work.

These reports were all given to the Captain
of each room who arranged and classified them,
At the weekly meeting of the pupils with the
teacher these reports were discussed.

A SCHOOL GARDEN

LESSON I

GARDEN PREPARATION

WEEDS

A weed is a plant in the wrong place. A pumpkin vine in a bed of onions might be considered a weed. Our experience with weeds has led us to believe that weeds are plants that have no use whatever a n d never will have any use. This is because we have not yet found the value and use of weeds.

Tomato plants were at one time considered weeds and by some people, their fruit w a s considered poisonous. Tomatoes h a v e now come to be a very

FIELD BINDWEED, MORNING-GLORY

valuable food because we have learned more about them. Not all weeds may become food but all weeds may become useful if we only knew how to use them.

Weeds, however, must be kept out of gardens because they will crowd out useful plants if both are allowed to grow together.

Before the garden is spaded or plowed, all coarse weeds should be pulled up and burned. If they are dug up or spaded up many of their roots will be cut

PINK FLEABANE
Common in moist ground from July to August

off and each part of the root left in the ground will likely grow again. Even when the weeds are pulled out, sometimes parts of the roots are broken off. These parts grow after the garden is started.

Sometimes the seeds of the weeds drop off before the weeds are removed from the garden and these seeds grow after the garden is started.

After the rubbish and weeds are removed, the ground should be well covered with well rotted stable

BEGGAR TICKS
Found in grain fields, near brooks, in barnyards, and low ground. Grows from 2 to 5 feet high

manure and then plowed or spaded to a depth of about six inches if the ground is hard. If the ground is loose or sandy, it may not be necessary to till it to such a depth.

After this work has been done the ground should be surface tilled or leveled with a rake or harrow. All weeds that have not been pulled out and that appear after the ground is surface tilled should be removed. Many of these weeds that have been turned down by the plow or spade will die because the sunlight cannot reach them. The purpose of removing the weeds is to keep them from robbing the vegetables of nourishment. Another very important purpose in tillage is to loosen the ground so that the fine roots of the vegetables can easily get down into the ground in their search for nourishment.

When the ground is surface tilled, some commercial fertilizer should be scattered over the ground and then surface tilled again.

HUMUS

Humus is decayed animal or vegetable matter such as rotted leaves or stable manure and is necessary to all growth of plant life. The soil in the forest is dark in color because it contains much humus. If we dig down in the ground until we get below the soil, we will generally find yellow clay. The difference between the soil and the clay is that the soil contains humus and the clay does not.

Soil will produce good crops during any season if some kind of commercial fertilizer is used. If, however, the soil is to have a permanent producing power it must have humus in it. Humus is the one thing that poor gardens need more than any other. In the middle west of the United States the soil is very deep because for hundreds of years the Mississippi river, which was at one time very much larger than it is now, brought into its valley a great deal of humus from the country over which the water of its upper course flowed. This humus settled in the great river valley and has been doing so for hundreds of years.

This is also the reason that any river valley is better growing land than the land that is higher.

The American people show very little knowledge of humus because they waste so much of it. We burn the leaves from our shade trees and the clippings from our lawns and do not seem to know that much of the waste material of the garbage can may be used as humus if saved. A pound of humus will produce sufficient wheat to make ten loaves of bread.

In every garden there should be a certain place where falling leaves, grass clippings, vegetable tops, fruit parings, and all other animal or vegetable material, which otherwise would be wasted, may be placed. This place may be hidden by a rose arbor or shrubbery of some kind so that it may not be unsightly. When this out-of-sight place is selected all material that will produce humus should be brought to this place and sufficient earth mixed with it to keep it moist. It will then rot and become very valuable for the garden. The decay of this animal or vegetable material may be hastened by spading or forking it over every fortnight. When it has sufficiently decayed to mix easily with the earth it should be spread on the garden. There will never be any good reason for poor gardens if this compost heap is given proper attention. Stable manure is also very valuable as humus but should not be exposed to the weather until it is placed on the garden because the rains and the hot sun take away much of its value.

SOIL

There are four general kinds of soil: humus soil, clay soil, sandy soil, and lime soil. We have learned that soil is the dark upper layer of the ground that contains humus. All soil must then contain humus. Some soils contain much more humus than others. The soil that contains a very great amount of humus is called humus soil. Clay soil contains a very great amount of clay, together with humus. Lime soil contains much lime, and sandy soil contains much sand.

A certain kind of soil will produce some crops much better than another kind. Because of this it is important to know what kind of soil we have in a certain garden or field which we wish to plant. If we do not know what soil we have we might plant a crop that could not easily be produced from such a soil.

It is impossible to change a sandy soil to a clay soil or a humus soil to a sandy soil. Lime, sand, or clay may be applied to a very small garden and by doing so we may change the character of the soil, but this is possible only on a very small garden. It could not be done with several acres.

DRAINAGE

No soil will produce a good crop if water is allowed to stay on the surface of the ground. In order that plants may grow well, the air must get into the earth and among the roots. The air cannot do this unless the water either sinks into the ground or is drained away. Air does not easily pass through water. Most ground will drain itself because of its slope. If it does not do this, it is then necessary to drain it. A wet garden or a wet field is always unproductive.

The ground may be drained in two ways; either by ditches, or underdraining. It is generally easy to dig ditches in the direction of the slope if there is a slope and to dig them deep enough to carry away all surplus water. If underdraining is used, more expense will be necessary. This is done very much like the draining by ditches except that tile are placed in the ditches and covered with earth. In ordinary gardens draining by ditches is all that will be necessary.

QUESTIONS

1. What is a weed?

2. Why do we consider weeds useless or harmful?

3. Explain how weeds should be removed in

the preparation of a garden and show why they should be removed in this way.

4. After great care is used in removing weeds why do they appear in the garden after it is planted?

5. Why should gardens be plowed or spaded, and how deep? Why so deep?

6. What is meant by surface tillage?

7. Why should fertilizer be placed on the garden before it is plowed?

8. Why is commercial fertilizer placed on the garden after it is plowed?

9. What is humus? What is soil?

10. Name the different kinds of soil and state why each is so called?

11. Why is the soil in the forest dark?

12. What is a compost heap?

13. How should a compost heap be cared for?

14. How should stable manure be kept until it is placed on the garden? Why?

15. Why is it important to know the kind of soil before planting?

16. Is it possible to change the kind of soil easily?

17. What is drainage and what is its purpose?

18. Why cannot plants grow when water lies on the top of the ground?

19. Describe the two ways in which ground may be drained.

20. What are tile and how are they put together in the ditch?

21. In what direction must the ditch be dug?

LESSON II

SEEDS

Grains of corn look very much alike but they are as different as the boys in any class. Some grains will grow and some will not grow. Some grains will produce good corn and some will produce very inferior corn. We cannot know everything about these grains unless we know something about their parents. If the grains come from large well developed ears of corn they will likely produce the same kind of ears if the plants are well cared for while they are growing. What is true of corn is also true of other seeds. It is very important that the seed we plant be good seed.

It is always wise to buy a variety of seed that has a name because greater care is generally used in the selection of such seed. These named varieties will probably cost more but they are worth more.

Some seeds will grow and others will not grow. It is always well to sprout several seeds from each seed package to determine how many of the seeds will grow so that when the seeds are planted, sufficient may be planted to allow for those that will not grow.

The seed is made up of three parts; the seed germ, the nourishment that is stored around the germ, and the covering. The germ in the grain of corn is the soft white part, the nourishment is the hard yellow part, and the covering is the thick skin in which the whole seed is enclosed. The germ is the part that starts growing but it must have some nourishment to keep it growing until its roots and leaves get large enough to bring it food. The outer covering is for protection only.

TESTING SEEDS

1. Place several layers of blotting paper, or some kind of heavy paper that will absorb moisture, in a fruit jar and thoroughly moisten with water. On this paper place several seeds that have been soaked in water for about twelve hours. Cover the jar with cardboards or other loose covering and make certain that the blotting paper is kept moist.

2. Fill a large glass tumbler or glass jar with water and tie over the top a layer of thin cloth. On this cloth place the seeds. The tumbler or jar should be kept sufficiently full of water to keep the cloth moist. Cover the seeds loosely with damp paper.

3. Place earth in a shallow box and over the earth place a thin cloth. The earth and the cloth must be kept saturated with moisture. On this cloth place the seeds. The seeds should then be covered with moist paper. This paper should be kept moist at all times while the seeds are sprouting.

Three things are necessary that plant life may grow well. These are light, heat, and moisture. Light is not essential that plants may grow. Potatoes may sprout and grow in a dark cellar, but light is essential that the plant may grow properly.

No plant can reach its proper growth without light. The light produces the green part of the plant and this green part of the plant does almost the same work for the plant that the stomach in the human body does for people. Although plants may start to grow without light, they cannot even do this without heat and moisture. Plants may have too much heat and moisture or they may have too little. Care should be used in germinating seeds that they do not get too cold or too hot and that they are not allowed to dry out or become suffocated by too much moisture.

During this sprouting time, it is the nourishment around the germ that makes it possible for the seed to sprout. If there is a great deal of nourishment around the germ as in the bean, the seed may grow until it is quite large without its roots supplying any nourishment from the ground. This is also true with plants that produce bulbs in the fall. They produce these bulbs in order that they may have a good start the next spring while their roots are getting nourishment from the ground.

QUESTIONS

1. Do all grains of corn produce well?
2. From what kind of ears should seed-corn be selected?
3. Is the selection of seed important? Why?
4. In selecting seed, is the knowledge of the parent seed of value?
5. Examine an ear of corn and discuss the merits of the grain for use as seed.
6. Name the different parts of the seed and give the purpose of each part.

7. How may good seed be selected?

8. What kind of seed should be bought? Why?

9. Why should seed be sprouted before it is planted?

10. Explain three ways in which seed may be sprouted.

11. Explain the purpose of the paper used in sprouting seed.

12. What should never be omitted in sprouting seed?

13. What things are necessary for plant growth?

14. What is the purpose of the green part of the plant? How is it produced?

15. What is the purpose of the nourishment that is found around the germ?

LESSON III

THE VALUE OF SEEDS

The purpose of seeds is to produce other plants like their parents. Before man began to cultivate plants, the seeds grew into plants like their parents. For many years efforts have been made to change the nature of many plants. Some have tried to make fruit larger and the plant smaller.

Some have tried to make the fruit seedless and of a better flavor. Some have even tried to change the shape and color of the fruit. These changes have been mostly brought about by grafting or budding. This is simply making the stalk of one plant grow on the stalk of another. Most cultivated plants have become so mingled with other kinds in this way that the seed may produce a plant like any one of its ancestors. Because of this the seeds which have been so produced are not used in planting. This is true of fruit trees, roses, and berries.

Although seeds seem to be produced solely for producing other plants, yet these seeds have become the most important of all foods. Among the most common seeds or fruit that have become commonly used as food are the berries, wheat, rice, corn, and oats.

Few seeds will germinate after they have become three or four years old. A very few seeds have been known, however, to germinate after fifty or sixty years but this cannot be depended on.

If seeds are to be picked from plants for planting, great care must be taken that these plants are not highly cultivated plants. We have learned that such seeds will probably produce a plant entirely different from the one from which the seed was taken. The corn, wheat, oats and other similar grains may be preserved and replanted the following year. In keeping these seeds for planting the following year it must be remembered that they must be kept in a warm dry place if they are to grow. If they are allowed to get damp and cold they will begin to decay and soon will be worthless.

QUESTIONS

1. What is the purpose of seeds?
2. Name two uses of seeds.
3. Name some fruits that have become seedless by cultivation.
4. What has been the purpose in attempts to change the character of plants?
5. Why will not all seeds produce plants like their parents?
6. How long may seeds be kept for planting?
7. How should seeds be kept if they are to be planted the following year?
8. Name four seeds that are used for food as well as for planting.

A HOME GARDEN IN WASHINGTON, D. C.

LESSON IV

EARLY PLANTING

If early vegetables are to be obtained from the garden, the seeds must be planted in a hotbed or in a protected or sheltered place before the weather is warm enough for them to be planted in the garden. Sufficient plants may be started in a hotbed at school to supply plants for any schoolroom, or a very carefully selected place on the south side of some building may be utilized where there will be some protection from the frost that might come after the plant has come up out of the ground. The purpose of the hotbed is to produce sufficient warmth for the sprouting seeds and at the same time protect from frost. This warmth is generally obtained from manure secured from some horse stable. The protection from frost is secured by placing glass over the sprouting seeds or plants. Care should be taken that this glass should be raised on warm days and lowered at night. This will give the plants warm air without chilling them.

An inexpensive plan to follow in making this hotbed is to dig a hole in the ground large enough to seat a large box which may be secured at some drygoods store at small expense. At least one

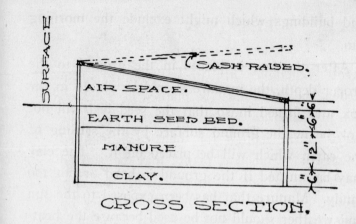

CROSS SECTION.

SURFACE

SASH RAISED.

AIR SPACE.

EARTH SEED BED.

MANURE

CLAY.

6"x 6"x 12"x 6"

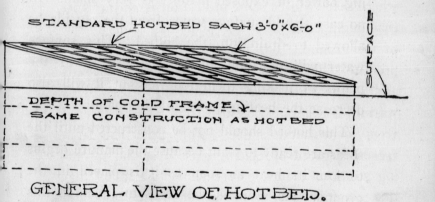

STANDARD HOTBED SASH 3'-0"x 6'-0"

SURFACE

DEPTH OF COLD FRAME
SAME CONSTRUCTION AS HOTBED

GENERAL VIEW OF HOTBED.

foot of the box should remain above the ground. The top should be so shaped as to allow a slope of six inches. This slope should face toward the south when the box is placed in the ground and should be so placed as to be free from shade trees and buildings which might exclude the morning sun.

After the box is placed in the ground to the proper depth, the manure should be placed in the box and firmed in so that the seed bed will not sink below the ground surface by the settling of the earth which will be placed on it. The clay may be omitted if the ground is hard or not too sandy. Manure that has been exposed to the sun and weather should not be used because the heating power of exposed manure is very small. In no case should surface water from the outside be allowed to drain into the hotbed. This surface water will not only hinder the growth of the plants by making them too wet but it will also decrease the heating power of the manure.

This hotbed should not be constructed until the seeds are ready to plant because the manure begins to lose its heat as soon as it is placed in the ground. As soon as the seeds are planted this heat is used by the plants in their growth and development.

Instead of using a box which extends to the bottom of the manure, boards may be used which extend only to the bottom of the seed bed. If boards are used, care should be taken that they are fastened firmly together at the corners so that they may not separate and admit too much cold air to the plants. The glass door or cover will not fit unless these corners are well fastened.

Old window frames that have no broken glass in them may be used for the glass door. On very cold nights this glass door should be closed and burlap or a blanket placed over it. Care must be taken that this burlap or blanket is removed in the morning and some air admitted as soon as danger from the cold night is passed.

QUESTIONS

1. What is necessary if early vegetables are to be obtained from a garden?

2. How may sufficient plants be started for a schoolroom?

3. Give an inexpensive plan to follow in making a hotbed.

4. What may be used instead of using a box which extends to the bottom of the manure?

LESSON V

THE HOTBED AND COLD FRAME

In northern regions the hotbed is necessary in order to get the plants started early. The covering may be made of cotton cloth instead of window glass. In more southern regions the cold frame may be used instead of the hotbed. The cold frame is similar to the hotbed except that no heating material such as manure is used. The window sash or cotton cloth is used solely to protect the plants from cold and in the cold frame the sun's rays furnish sufficient heat.

Great care should be taken that the plants are well ventilated. This may be done by raising the door slightly during the early part of the day. The plants should be watered at the same time the hotbed or cold frame is ventilated. This will give the plants time to evaporate the water from their leaves before night. About the middle of the afternoon the door of the hotbed should be closed. By doing this the soil will have a chance to become warm before night.

During warm days, the plants will get very warm from the sun's rays shining through the glass. The door should always be raised during such days.

Before the seed is planted, great care should be taken that the soil which is placed in the hotbed is of excellent quality and that it has been thoroughly heated so as to kill all bugs or insects or eggs which they may have laid in the soil. This may be done by placing the soil in some pan or vessel and placing it in a hot oven for about one hour. This soil should consist of three-fourths humus and one-fourth sand.

QUESTIONS

1. Draw a cross-section of a hotbed or cold frame.

2. Explain how a hotbed may be made.

3. Why is manure placed in the hotbed?

4. Why should manure that has been exposed to the sun and the weather not be used in the hotbed?

5. How may the surface water be kept out of the hotbed? Why should it be kept out?

6. Why should the manure be firmed down before the seed bed is placed in the hotbed?

7. What kind of a door should the hotbed have?

8. How may the hotbed be protected during cold nights?

9. Why should the plants be ventilated and how?

10. How does a cold frame differ from a hotbed?

11. When should the plants be exposed to the air? Why?

12. When should the door of the hotbed be closed? Why?

13. How should the soil be prepared before it is placed in the hotbed?

LESSON VI

PLANTING

Three important rules should be followed in planting seeds:

1. Plant seeds in season.

2. Plant good seeds.

3. Plant the seeds in straight rows.

The proper season for planting seed in one section of the country may not be correct for another. Some seeds will rot in the ground if cold weather should come after they are planted. Some seeds grow well in spite of some cold weather. Some seeds grow better if planted in the fall of the year.

It is wasted time and effort to plant seeds that are not known to be good. This may be determined by sprouting the seeds and cannot easily be determined in any other way. It is always better to buy seeds that have a particular name because by doing so one can be assured of their being selected in a more careful way.

Seeds should always be planted in straight rows. The soil should always be firmed down after the seeds are planted. These rows should be about two inches apart in the hotbed or cold frame. When these plants are transplanted to the garden, they should again be planted in straight rows, but sufficiently far apart for the plants to grow properly. It is necessary that the rows be straight in order that the plants may have an equal chance to grow well, and that the weeds may be easily removed and the soil well cultivated.

After the seeds are planted, care should be taken that the ground should be moist, not wet, until the seeds are well started.

The size and kind of seeds will determine to what depth the seeds should be planted. If the seeds are very small they should not be planted deep. If they are planted deep they will probably rot before they reach the surface. It should always be remembered that young plants should not be given too much water because the air must get to the roots if the plants are to grow well.

These young plants should be transplanted just

A VEGETABLE GARDEN PLANTED IN ROWS

as soon as they can be handled easily or as soon as they begin to crowd each other. During this transplanting, the roots must not be broken or crushed and they should be planted in their new bed in as nearly the same position as they grew before transplanting.

If the plants are sensitive to the heat of the sun, such as cabbage, they should be protected in some way for about two days after they are transplanted. After their roots have become attached to the soil and are able to furnish nourishment for the plant the protection may be removed. When plants are transplanted they should be placed a little deeper in the ground than they were before they were transplanted.

QUESTIONS

1. Name three rules which should be followed in planting seeds.

2. Why may not all plants be planted at the same season?

3. Why should the seeds be good?

4. What precaution should be taken in buying seed?

5. Why should the seeds be planted in straight rows?

6. In what condition should the ground be kept after the plants are transplanted?

7. How deep should seeds be planted?

8. What will be the result if the seeds are planted too deep?

9. What precaution should be taken with the roots when transplanting?

10. What precaution should be given plants after transplanting? Why?

* * * * * * *

Every garden, however small, should have at least ten vegetables in it. A very much larger number should be planted in larger gardens. Ten, at least, should be selected from the following ones outlined in this text.

A few very important things should be kept prominently in mind in selecting and planting vegetables in the garden. These are rich soil, frequent cultivation, and protection from insects.

LESSON VII

INJURIOUS INSECTS

There are two kinds of insects which do most damage to garden crops. One of these bites the leaves and causes them to have a ragged appearance. The cabbage worm is a good example of this kind. The other kind has a very sharp tongue or beak which it pushes down into the leaf. With this beak or tube it sucks the sap from the plant, which soon withers and in many cases dies. The black squash bug is a good example of this kind.

There are many other pests which do much damage to plants. Some bite the roots, some eat

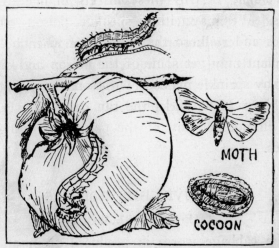

BOLL-WORM

It eats green tomatoes, beans and peas. The boll-worm destroys the green boll of the cotton plant, also green vegetables.

the entire stem off just under the ground and some destroy the pollen of the flower when in bloom. Most of the injurious insects, however, either eat the leaf or suck the sap.

It is necessary for the gardener, if he is to protect his garden, to destroy these pests as soon as they appear. He must not only destroy the insects, but in doing so he must not destroy the plant or injure it in any way.

Many of these insects may be caught and killed, but there are so many of them and they are, in many cases, so small that it is little use to attempt to catch them.

We may destroy these insects in one of two ways. We may either sprinkle poison on the leaves and stalk so that the insect when he bites the plant may get some of the poison and die, or we may sprinkle his body with something that will kill him. If he sucks the sap only, it is certain he will not get any of the poison by biting the leaves.

THE FIVE CHIEF ROBBERS
THE CABBAGE WORM

The cabbage worm is produced from an egg just as little chicks are, except that the cabbage worm requires only one week, from the time the egg is laid for it to hatch, and it requires three weeks for the little chick to hatch and during this time the eggs must have care.

The mother of this cabbage worm was a white butterfly. Many of these white butterflies may be seen flitting about among the cabbage plants on bright spring mornings. This is when she lays her eggs on the cabbage leaves. After she lays her eggs she does not seem to give them any care at all, but leaves them to be hatched by the heat of the sun. When the cabbage worm first comes out of the egg it is a tiny green worm or caterpillar. It begins almost at once to nibble at the green leaves on which the eggs were left by the mother butterfly.

In about ten days it has become too large for its clothes. It then throws off its old skin, or molts, and keeps on eating holes in the cabbage leaves. It changes its clothes, or molts, several times during its stay on the cabbage leaf, which is about four or five weeks. It now seems to want to hide itself as though it were conscious of having destroyed the plant. It may crawl down to the underside of the leaf or to the ground. Here it molts for the last time and wraps itself up in a mass of fine silk threads, which it makes. It is now called a chrysalis and sleeps for about one week. It then awakens into a white butterfly like its mother.

The chrysalis is not so easily found as the worm because it tries to find a concealed place where it may grow into a butterfly without being disturbed. If these butterflies had been caught when they first came into the garden there would have been no cabbage worms. Because it is almost impossible to catch so many of these butterflies, we must then do something to destroy the worms before they kill or ruin the plants.

THE TOMATO WORM

The tomato worm is a sort of half-cousin to the cabbage worm. Their mothers are not alike in appearance, but they both fly through the air. Although it is difficult to catch the white butterflies that lay the cabbage worm eggs, yet it is still more difficult to catch the great hawk-moth that lays the eggs from which the tomato worms are hatched. It is more difficult because the hawk-moth is not easily seen. She comes around the garden in the evenings when the light is not good. She visits other plants as well as tomato plants. However, she seems to like tomato plants best. She lays her eggs in the evenings in much the same way as the white butterfly. Her eggs look just like a small bit of light colored jelly. In a few days these eggs hatch into a large grayish-green worm with a great horn on the rear end of its body. This tomato worm, like the cabbage worm, lives by eating leaves. Its life history is short and is much like that of the cabbage worm. It crawls to the ground and into the soil, where it molts and changes to a chrysalis. In the cold latitudes it remains dormant until the following spring, when it reappears as a hawk-moth.

THE CORN WORM

If the ears of corn are examined carefully while they are growing on the stalk, a little round hole may be found on some of the ears from the outside of the husk to the kernels within. If the husk is removed it will be noticed that much of the silk has been eaten, also many of the kernels. These are the tracks of some robber.

The name of this robber is the corn worm. It was hatched from an egg just as were the cabbage worm and the tomato worm. The mother of this worm was a brownish-yellow moth which visited the garden in the early summer when the ears were beginning to form.

WARNING

THE EUROPEAN CORN BORER

**This pest attacks CORN, POTATOES, OATS, FODDER AND GARDEN CROPS
and has recently been found in the United States
where it is doing great damage.**

THERE IS GRAVE DANGER OF THIS SERIOUS FOREIGN PEST BEING BROUGHT INTO CANADA.

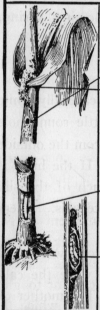

HOW TO RECOGNIZE IT

Holes in the stalks of the above mentioned plants with sawdust-like material issuing from them indicate the presence of the borer or caterpillar. In the case of corn broken tassels also show where the borer is at work.

If the infested stems are split open the caterpillars will be found at work. These are often found just above the roots.

The insect spends the winter as a caterpillar in old stalks of corn or other food plants and changes to a reddish-brown pupa late in the spring. The pupa soon turns into a moth.

Illustrations reproduced by courtesy of the Bureau of Entomology, U. S. Department of Agriculture.

A robber that attacks and kills many food plants—the corn borer

This mother moth on her visit to the garden laid some eggs on the blades of corn, which were hatched in five or six days into caterpillars. These caterpillars seemed to know how to reach the ends of the ears of corn. Here it was they began to eat the silk and to dig their way into the ear. After they find their way into the ear they make their home here for several weeks and grow very fat. When they have grown to about one inch in length they eat a hole through the husk to the out-side. It now crawls to the ground like the cab-bage worm and the tomato worm, and develops into a chrysalis or pupa. It finally awakens as a brownish-yellow moth.

PLANT LICE

Plant lice are not much like the corn worm. They are not very particular about the kind of plants they attack. They will attack any kind of a plant on which they can get sufficient to eat. Plant lice are different from many insects because they do not bite or eat the leaves of the plant on which they live. They push their beaks or tongues into the plant or leaf and suck the sap which lies underneath the surface of the leaf and bark. Trees, shrubs, flowers, and vegetables are very often injured by these lice. After they begin to

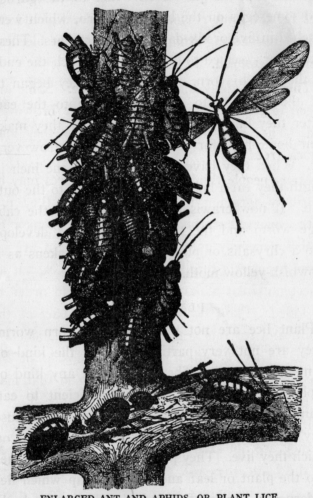

**ENLARGED ANT AND APHIDS, OR PLANT LICE,
VERY COMMON ON PLANTS**
The Aphids secrete a sweet fluid called honeydew, of which ants
are very fond

suck the sap, the plant soon withers and dies. It dies for the same reason that an animal would die if it were bleeding from a wound and the bleeding were not stopped.

There are many kinds of plant lice. Some are green in color and others are black or brownish-red. They may attack rose bushes or they may attack trees.

Many people think these little creatures may be killed by spraying the plant on which they live with poison, but this is not true. Arsenate of lead is generally used to spray plants that are injured by insects that bite or eat the leaves, but an insect must eat a part of this poison in order to be killed. Plant lice do not eat any part of the plant, and for this reason this poison will not kill them. They get their food from inside of the plant and do not get any of the poison that may be placed by spraying on the outside.

Plant lice increase in numbers very rapidly, and if they are not killed very soon after they appear on the plant, they will cause the plant to die very quickly. The parent louse gives birth to a great number of baby lice, and these baby lice grow to their full size in about eight days. These young lice then give birth to more baby lice, and very soon the plant is covered with these insects.

These insects are not hard to kill if one knows how to go about it. Since they do not eat anything, but simply suck the sap from the inside, we cannot feed them poison. These insects that suck the sap seem to be very sensitive if certain kinds of poison touches the outside of their bodies. If a solution of nicotine, one teaspoonful of nicotine sulphate to a gallon of water, is used as a spray and a small particle of this solution touches them they will die. This solution will cling to the leaves of the plant better if a piece of soap about the size of an egg is dissolved with the solution. Care should be taken that a fine spray is used, so that all parts of the plant may be reached, the under side of the leaves as well as the upper side.

Plants should be sprayed with this solution about once every five days for about three weeks if all of these lice are to be destroyed. This poison may be used for all kinds of insects that suck the sap but do not bite the leaves. After the lice are killed, the plant will recover if it is not too badly injured. Ants use the aphids as "milk cows." They stake them with their antennæ and reserve a sweet substance which the aphids secrete.

THE SQUASH BUG

The squash bug is much like plant lice. It gets its food in the same way, but it is much larger than plant lice. This bug has wings and is generally black in color.

These bugs lay their eggs in small clusters on the leaves of the squash, melon, or cucumber vine and are hatched in about two weeks. In about one week after the young bug is hatched it molts, or sheds, its skin. They do this several times before they are full grown. When they become almost full grown, they grow wings just like their parents. Very soon after they are hatched they begin to suck the sap. As soon as they are full grown, which takes only a few weeks, they lay eggs on the leaves just like the ones from which they were hatched.

The leaves on which these bugs live soon wither and die, much like the plants on which the plant lice live. These bugs are destroyed in the same way as are the plant lice.

Squash bugs have a peculiar habit of hiding at night under leaves or loose stones near the vine on which they live. If these hiding places are examined very early in the morning, these bugs may easily be seen and killed before they get back to their feeding places.

There is a distinct difference between the squash bug and the squash or cucumber beetle. These beetles are striped or spotted and are very different in their habits because they eat and bite the leaves.

For these insects that bite or eat the leaves, a solution of arsenate of lead, about one ounce to a gallon of water, is the best poison to rid the plants of these pests.

If the plants are powdered with a fine powder of arsenate of lead while the dew is still on the

BOY AND SUMMER SQUASHES

leaves, these bugs will get some of the poison just about as well as if the solution were used. This poison is very dangerous and should be carefully guarded, as it will kill people just as it kills the beetles.

QUESTIONS

1. Name the two kinds of insects that injure plants.

2. Name two examples of each kind.

3. Are there any other than these two kinds of insects that harm plants?

4. Explain how these insects injure plants.

5. Why are these insects not caught and killed before they injure the plants?

6. Name the five chief robbers of the garden.

7. How does the cabbage worm get into the garden?

8. How long does it require for the cabbage worm to hatch from the egg?

9. How does the cabbage worm harm the cabbage?

10. Name two important things which happen to the cabbage worm during his lifetime.

11. What is a chrysalis?

12. Where does the cabbage worm go before it turns into a chrysalis?

13. From what kind of a parent does the tomato worm come?

14. Describe the appearance of this worm.

15. How does its life history differ from that of the cabbage worm?

16. What is the nature and color of the mother of the tomato worm?

17. Explain the operations of the corn worm.

18. When may the mother of the corn worm be seen?

19. What is the color and size of the corn worm?

20. How does it injure the corn?

21. What are plant lice and on what plants do they live?

22. Explain how they get their food.

23. What is the appearance of these plant lice?

24. Explain how quickly they mature.

25. Distinguish between the squash bug and the squash beetle.

26. How does the squash bug differ from the tomato worm? The corn worm?

27. What causes the plant, on which the squash bug lives, to die?

28. How may each of the five robbers mentioned be killed?

LESSON VIII

THINNING FRUIT AND PLANTS

Everyone has noticed that some trees, such as apple trees and peach trees, have a large crop some years and other years have no fruit at all. This may be caused by one of two things. Late frosts may kill the young bud before it is in blossom. These frosts may not kill the bud entirely, but may so weaken the stem of the fruit that it will fall to the ground when the fruit begins to grow. The ground may be seen strewn with this partly grown fruit long before the fruit that remains on the tree is ripe.

If the frost does not injure the bud nor the stem, the fruit may grow until it is mature, but because there is such a large crop on the tree none of it can develop into full size. The tree cannot get sufficient nourishment to supply all of its fruit with the proper amount of food material. We may then expect the fruit to be small and imperfect. The tree will make a great effort through its roots and leaves to bring enough nourishment from the ground and air to perfect and ripen its fruit, but the task is too great. When the time for the next crop of fruit has come, the tree has so exhausted itself in this great effort that no fruit may appear. To avoid this condition, the fruit should be thinned when it begins to develop so that the tree can properly care for what is left on the tree after the proper amount has been removed. By thinning the fruit in this way, as many bushels of fruit will be picked from the tree as though the entire amount of the crop were allowed to develop, and it will be a finer quality.

In the garden many more seeds are planted than will develop well unless they are thinned and transplanted. It is easier and better to plant more seeds than we want plants, and then thin them, than it is to replant if some seeds fail to grow.

Some seeds may easily be transplanted, but others cannot be transplanted. Onions and beets may be transplanted with good results, but corn cannot be transplanted. By transplanting the young plants we save much time in the spring, as many of the plants may first be planted in hotbeds long before the weather is fit to plant them in the garden.

Two plants cannot grow in a place where there is nourishment for only one. Two apples cannot grow on a twig which is able to produce food for only one. The roots must have room to spread out in search for nourishment and the leaves must have room to get the sunlight.

Transplanting must be done while the plants are young. If the plants are allowed to grow until their roots develop, they will become entangled with the roots of another plant, and one cannot be easily removed without tearing the roots of the other.

QUESTIONS

1. What causes fruit crops to be uncertain?

2. What causes the fruit to fall to the ground before it matures?

3. Why is the fruit of a tree that is loaded with fruit not so well developed as the fruit of a tree not so loaded?

4. How can this difficulty be corrected?

5. Why should more seeds be planted in the garden than are wanted for plants?

6. When should plants be transplanted? Why?

7. What plants may be transplanted easily?

8. Why should plants not be close together?

9. Give a special reason for using the hotbed.

10. Name one plant that cannot be easily transplanted.

LESSON IX

THE CODLING MOTH

Some moths are very beautiful and their caterpillars are either useful or harmless. Among these is the Cecropia moth. There are many moths that are not beautiful and some of these produce caterpillars that are very destructive. The beauty of the moth, however, is no indication that the caterpillar will be useful or harmless. The moth may be beautiful and its caterpillar destructive, or the moth may not be so beautiful and yet may produce a useful caterpillar.

The codling moth is a small brown moth which flies about generally at night. In the spring, when the apple trees are in bloom, it will visit the apple blossoms and lay its eggs on the young apples near the center of the blossom. Very soon there will hatch from these eggs, larvæ, or apple worms, which at once begin to eat their way into the apples. They will always enter the apple from the blossom end. In making this burrow, the larva uses what it digs out of the apple as food. After digesting this pulp, it will push the waste material out behind it. If we examine an apple, into which one of these apple worms has burrowed, we will generally find some of this waste material at the mouth of the burrow.

It will continue to dig until it reaches the seed which it especially likes to eat. Here it will remain until it has matured, which will not be until late in the summer. It lines its burrow with a thin layer of silk which it spins as it goes. It lives in the center of the apple, well protected from birds and any other enemy which may destroy it. Even man cannot reach it without destroying the apple in which it lives.

When this apple worm is mature it measures from a half inch to one inch in length and is grayish-white in color. It has twelve segments and, for about two months after it is hatched, it has dark spots on each segment. It has two real legs on each of the three segments just back of the head. On all of the other segments except the last one, are what seem to be legs, but are called pro-legs, and will disappear when the apple worm changes to a moth. On the last segment there is only one pro-leg. This is sometimes called the prop-leg and is used to push the apple worm along as it digs through the apple.

Another larva, much like the appleworm, is sometimes found on apple trees. This is the plum curculio and may easily be distinguished from the appleworm because it has no legs.

When the apple worm has become full grown, it will dig another burrow out to the surface of the apple. It digs this burrow out to the side of the apple and does not go out at the stem nor through the same hole which it used on entering. When it reaches the surface, it may seal up the opening and remain inside for a few days. When it finally gets ready to enter the outside world, all it needs to do is to push out the material with which it has already sealed the opening.

On reaching the outside of the apple, it seems to know that it is exposed to birds and is in great danger. The birds which are especially fond of the apple worm as food are the woodpeckers and chickadees. The nuthatches also like to eat them. To avoid being in danger very long, the apple worm will hurry down the tree and hide under the loose bark. It very often spins a strand of silk and on this swings down to a lower part of the tree where there is loose bark, or near where it wants to hide. Here it remains until spring when it makes its cocoon and changes from a larva into a pupa. In this pupa stage it gradually changes into a moth and finally comes out of its cocoon in time to lay eggs on the apple blossoms.

Should the apple fall from the tree before the larva has left the apple, it will not change its plan except that, when it comes from the apple, it may seek shelter on the ground under a leaf, stone, or log. If the tree is not too far away, however, it will probably return to the tree and seek shelter under the loose bark.

By eating at the center of the apple it keeps the apple from growing large. It may so weaken the apple that it will drop from the tree before it is ripe. It also causes the apple to decay. If an apple, in which the apple worm has been working, is examined it will be noticed that the apple decays very readily where the worm has entered and also where it has left the apple. Apples that are small, or have started to decay, are not easily sold in the market and, because of this, are either not offered for sale or are sold at a much reduced price and for much less than good apples

During recent years, a great effort has been made by farmers and fruit growers to destroy this pest. The first precaution which should be taken is to destroy the larvae which conceal themselves under the bark of the tree. This may be done, before the pupa develops into a moth in the spring, by removing the loose bark from the trunk of the tree with a garden rake. This loose bark and larvae should be carefully collected and burned. By doing this there will not be so many moths to lay eggs on the apple blossoms.

It may be impossible to secure all of these larvae by this process and some may escape, develop into moths, and produce more apple worms. These may escape either by hiding well in the tree beyond the reach of the rake or they may come from apples that fell to the ground, and may have remained concealed under the leaves.

These must be reached in some way before the next season's crop is destroyed. To do this the larvae must be destroyed after they hatch from the eggs which are laid on the young apples, but before they burrow into the apple. This may be accomplished by spraying the trees with arsenate of lead solution just before the petals of the apple blossoms drop off. This spraying should be done with a very fine spray to make certain that all of the blossoms will be reached. This will kill the larvae before they have a chance to injure the apples, because arsenate of lead solution, when sprayed on vegetation, will kill all insects that eat or bite the leaves or fruit. In the case of the apple worm, it is very important that this spraying should be done at precisely the right time. After the larva has burrowed into the apple, spraying is useless. The spraying should start just as the petals begin to fall and should be completed before the petals have all left the tree.

Millions of bushels of apples are destroyed every year in the United States and Canada by this apple worm. In the latitude of Ohio there are generally two broods each season.

QUESTIONS

1. Describe the appearance of the codling moth.

2. Where does it lay its eggs?

3. What does the larva do when it first comes from the egg?

4. What is the appearance of this larva?

5. In what ways does this larva injure the fruit?

6. Where does this larva spend the winter?

7. What other larva may injure the apples?

8. How many broods are there of the apple worm each year?

9. Explain when and how the apple worm may be destroyed.

10. What birds aid in reducing the number of the apple worms?

LESSON X

THE WHITE-MARKED TUSSOCK MOTH

The tussock moth is a native of America. Among all insert life, this moth is one of our greatest enemies. In sections of the country where it has not been molested, it has done even more damage than the codling moth. It does not attack fruit like the codling moth caterpillar, or apple worm, but it destroys the foilage. It is not very particular as to what kind of tree it attacks so long as the tree is not a conifer. It seems to be particularly fond of the leaves of shade trees.

It is now being carefully watched by the departments of agriculture in the various states and provinces, and its progress over the country has been checked. In some of the New England states, in New York, in Pennsylvania, and southward along the Atlantic coast states, it has destroyed millions of trees. Its progress seems to be toward the west and only in recent years has it done any damage west of the Mississippi river.

The male moth is dark in color with a few slight markings on its front wings. Its antennae are well feathered and curved in much the same shape as a cow's horns. The upper segments of its front legs are also feathered. It has two pairs of wings. The front pair have a width of about one inch when they are extended.

The female is very different from her mate. She has no wings and her body is oval in shape, being about three-fourths of an inch long and about half as wide as it is long. The bagworm and the tussock moth are the only shade tree insects which have wingless females.

The male and female moths come from the cocoons after having been in the cocoons, in the pupa stage, about two weeks. Within a day or two after they come from the cocoons, the female begins to lay her eggs. She will lay her eggs in a cluster which she fastens to the cocoon. This female does not seem to have any other purpose in life than to lay eggs. She does not even eat and as soon as her eggs are laid, she dies.

From two to four generations of these moths develop each year, one generation generally remains in the egg stage over winter and hatches out in April. These winter eggs are laid in September, and may be laid in the early part of October if the weather remains warm.

During the larva stage, which is the period between hatching and entering the cocoon, the larva molts five times. As soon as the larva hatches from the egg, it begins to eat the under surface of the leaf. By the time it is fully developed, the entire leaf will be devoured, with possibly the exception of the stem and the midrib.

The larvae migrate from one tree to another. When the leaves have been eaten from one tree they will either spin a slender strand of silk, as does the appleworm, and swing to the ground or they will crawl down the tree and move on to the next tree. In this manner they will soon defoliate an entire park or row of shade trees.

This larva stage continues for about a month or six weeks. When the larva has become fully developed, it has long barbed hairs on its body and a tuft of what looks like cotton appears on each of the fourth, fifth, sixth, and seventh seg-

.nents along its back. Two long tufts of stiff
hairs extend from the first segment back of its
head and seem to serve as antennae. Another
stiff tuft of hair extends backward from the
twelfth or last segment. These barbed hairs produce a stinging sensation if they come into contact with the skin of people. In this particular,
they serve as weapons of defense for the larvae.
As soon as the larva is mature, it spins its cocoon
and in this warm nest it passes through the pupa
stage which requires about two weeks.

During the process of building the cocoon,
many of the barbed hairs on the body of the larva
become entangled with the silk of the cocoon and
are pulled out. The removal of these hairs great-
ly changes the appearance of the larva.

The cocoons are most frequently fastened to
the bark of the tree near the ground, although they
may be fastened to any convenient support, such as
posts or brush, which may be near the tree on
which it has been feeding.

The best method of ridding a community of this
pest is to spray the trees frequently with arsenate
of lead solution. This should be begun as soon
as the larvae have hatched from the eggs. A band
of cotton may be tied around the trees that have

not been affected. This will keep the larvae from ascending the tree. The female does not wander about after she lays her eggs, and cannot fly, being wingless. She soon dies, so that the trees cannot be injured by any form of this pest except the larvae which crawl up the tree.

QUESTIONS

1. Describe the appearance of the tussock moth.

2. What difference exists between the appearance of the male and the female?

3. How long does the pupa remain in the cocoon?

4. How soon after the female moth comes from the cocoon does she begin to lay eggs?

5. What becomes of the female moth after she lays her eggs?

6. When do the first eggs hatch each season?

7. How many times does the larva molt?

8. How does the larva of the tussock moth injure vegetation?

9. What does the larva do after it has reached maturity?

10. How long does the larva stage continue?

11. Describe the appearance of the larva.

12. Does the larva have weapons of defense?

13. Where are the cocoons fastened?

14. What is the best remedy for this pest?

LESSON XI

THE FALL WEBWORM

The fall webworm, like the tussock moth, is a native of America but is more generally distributed over the country. It is found in almost all parts of the United States, with possibly the exception of the northwest where it has just recently begun to appear.

The webworm feeds on the leaves of almost all kinds of trees. The moth is white in color, but may have small dark spots on its fore wings. It is about one inch across when its wings are extended. The moth flies about at night and lays its eggs on the leaves of some tree. This tree is generally some shade or ornamental tree. It may lay as many as three hundred eggs on one leaf.

South of the latitude of New York City there will probably appear two broods in one season. When the larvae hatch from these eggs they live and feed in colonies. Each colony spins its own web. This web may include a very large limb of the tree and serves as a protection against birds and other enemies while the larvae are feeding on the leaves. These larvae will remain in this web until they are mature. They will then crawl down the tree and spin their cocoons. The second brood of the webworm appears during the latter part of August or first of September. This second brood is, in some localities, more destructive than the first one.

The webworm, like the larva of the tussock moth, has many stiff hairs on its body. These hairs on the webworm are more evenly distributed over the entire body and do not appear in tufts as they do on the larva of the tussock moth. These hairs give the webworm a very rough appearance. The body of the webworm has twelve segments as do most larvae and may be either dark or light in color. The hairs, however, are generally light in color and often become entangled in the web which the larvae spin around the limb where they are feeding. The cocoons are composed of silk and the hairs from the body of the larvae and present a very rough appearance on the bark of the tree. These cocoons may sometimes be found on some of the small twigs of the tree as well as on the trunk.

The webworm may be destroyed in three ways. The cocoons may be collected during the winter and burned. The trees may be sprayed with arsenate of lead solution. The webs may be burned by using a torch of some kind before the larvae have reached maturity. To make certain that good results may be obtained, all three methods should be used. The female webworm moth, unlike the female tussock moth, is a good flier and cannot be kept out of the trees by wrapping cotton around the trunk. If one cocoon is destroyed during the winter, hundreds of eggs will not be laid by the moth which would have come from this cocoon. It may be impossible to find all of the cocoons, but by properly spraying the trees just before the larvae have been hatched from the eggs, many more will be destroyed. Should some escape, their location may easily be determined by the web which they spin around their colony while they destroy the leaves.

QUESTIONS

1. In what ways is the webworm larva like the larva of the tussock moth?

2. Describe the appearance of the moth of the webworm.

3. Where is the webworm found?

4. What damage does it do?

5. How can its location be determined?

6. Why does it spin a web?

7. Where and when are the eggs laid?

8. How many broods of the webworm each season?

9. In what particular does the female of the webworm moth differ from the female of the tussock moth?

10. Name three ways by which the webworm may be destroyed.

LESSON XII

THE GRASSHOPPER

The grasshopper lives in fields where it can get grass or herbage to eat. It is a good representative of a large class of insects which have protection by having the same color as their surroundings. It is able to escape from many of its enemies by its great ability to jump. If an athlete could jump as far as the grasshopper, in proportion to his size, he could exceed the world's record in the broad jump and do it with very little effort. The athlete, however, cannot jump like the grasshopper because he is not constructed so well for jumping. The hind legs of the grasshopper are very long and strong. The femur, or upper part of the hind leg, is largely made up of large hard muscles which seem to be thoroughly woven together. The tibia, or second joint of the hind leg, is about as long as the femur but does not seem to have any muscle. The foot is composed of a sharp spike on the heel and sharp claws on the toes. When the grasshopper jumps it brings the femur and the tibia of each hind leg close together and adjusts its spiked heels so that it will not slip. When it is ready, its hind legs straighten as suddenly as the discharge of a gun and the grasshopper is thrown forward with great force.

The grasshopper, like moths and butterflies, has six legs. The front two are shortest and the two hind legs are longer than the entire body of the grasshopper. The grasshopper can walk and fly as well as jump. It can walk up a very steep surface or a blade of grass by the aid of very small hairs which are located between its toes and which secrete a sticky fluid as it walks. The grasshopper flies only when it desires to make a longer journey than it can make by jumping.

The grasshopper has two large compound eyes and a single eye in the center of its forehead. It has two pairs of jaws. It grasps the leaf or blade of grass, which it may desire to eat, with its front feet just like a dog holds a bone.

The grasshopper seems to have two pairs of wings but, if we examine it carefully, we will find that the outside pair are not used in flying, but are simply covers for the real wings which are underneath. These wing covers are held straight in the air when it flies. It does not fly very far, however, unless it finds little to eat and is forced to migrate to another part of the country. During this migration, grasshoppers will make their journey by flying high in the air.

The Carolina locusts have dark brown or black wings with yellow edges and the common grasshopper has gray wings.

The antennae of the grasshopper are kept very clean and serve the same purpose as antennae of most insects, by giving information concerning the things with which it comes in contact. Although these antennae do not seem so important nor so useful to the grasshopper as they do in the case of the ant, yet they are always kept very alert and are in continuous use.

One of the most interesting features of the grasshopper is its breathing. Its abdomen is constructed in segments with one fan-like fold, or crease, extending lengthwise on each side, on each of which can easily be seen a spiracle or breathing pore on each side. When the grasshopper breathes, it compresses its abdomen by folding and unfolding these fan-like creases, thus forcing the air in and out of these spiracles.

Its ears are found on the first segment of the abdomen under the wings, one being located on each side. They look to be small circular plates or sounding boards.

The female may easily be distinguished from the male by her ovipositor, which is a tube extending backward from the end of the abdomen. With this ovipositor she deposits her eggs in the ground or in the soft decayed wood of some tree. She closes this opening to the eggs with a kind of glue so that they may not easily be found by an enemy.

Grasshoppers do not pass through the larva stage after they come from the egg, as do apple worms or webworms, but are small grasshoppers when they are hatched. They look very much like their mature ancestors except that their heads, like babies' heads, seem to large for their bodies and the real wings are outside of the wing covers.

Grasshoppers generally spend the winter in the egg stage and hatch out in the spring.

Grasshoppers, like flies, seem to spend much of their time in cleaning themselves and they do it in much the same way.

The sounds made by grasshoppers vary. Some species produce a low heavy sound by rubbing the tibia and femur of the hind legs together. Other species, including the locust, produce a shrill sound by rubbing their legs against their wing covers.

The greatest enemies of the grasshopper are the birds, from which they can escape only by concealing themselves or by jumping. The grasshopper is not very successful in its effort to escape by jumping, because birds can easily overtake them in their flight. The grasshopper uses its jaws, when possible, to defend itself against its enemies. It also sends forth a brown acrid fluid from its mouth which has an offensive odor. These weapons of defense seem to protect it sufficiently to enable it to multiply very rapidly in many sections of the country. In very few instances is anything done to reduce the number of grasshoppers, so widely distributed are they and so difficult to reach. The most effective remedy is to plow the ground where they have been plentiful and where they have probably deposited their eggs. This plowing should be done before the eggs hatch in the spring. In the middle west, especially in Kansas and Nebraska, grasshoppers have been known to appear in such vast numbers as to darken the sun in their flight. This has not been a frequent occurrence, but such large numbers have been known to eat up all farm vegetation over large areas.

QUESTIONS

1. What does the grasshopper eat and where does it live?

2. How may it escape from its enemies?

3. How is the grasshopper able to jump so far?

4. Describe the hind feet of the grasshopper.

5. How does the grasshopper breathe?

6. What kind of eyes does the grasshopper have and where are they located?

7. Where may its ears be found?

8. How is the grasshopper able to crawl up a steep surface?

9. Describe the wings of the grasshopper.

10. How may the female be distinguished from the male?

11. Where does the female lay her eggs?

12. How does the grasshopper produce sound?

13. What weapons of defense does the grasshopper have?

LESSON XIII

THE CRICKET

The cricket resembles the grasshopper and the katydid in many ways. It can jump almost as far as the grasshopper because it is constructed in much the same way. In color the cricket is a glossy black. The palpi are little appendages which are located around the cricket's mouth and serve as tongues to enable the cricket to taste what it eats. The two larger ones are located just above the smaller ones. It also has a pair of very long antennae which it is very careful to keep clean.

The hind legs of the cricket are well adapted for their purpose. The upper part of the hind leg, which we may call the thigh, or femur, is very strong and muscular. The part next to this, which is called the tibia, is also very strong but is not so muscular as the femur nor so delicate as the tibia of the grasshopper. Instead of the spike which we find on the heel of the grasshopper, there are several, five in number, on the heel of the cricket. These spikes serve for the cricket the same purpose as do the spiked shoes for the athlete. The claws, which serve as toes, and the spines, which are found along the foot, enable the cricket to avoid slipping when it jumps and also enables it to run well through the grass, weeds, and leaves.

The cricket is not equipped with sticky pads on its feet like the grasshopper and the katydid and, because of this, it cannot climb so well. It has short wing covers and what seems to have been wings underneath these covers. It seems to have outgrown its wings just as the horse has outgrown its toes and they now no longer appear. However, these wing covers are not useless. Near the base of the wing covers, and on the inside, is a hard part called the scraper. When the cricket chirps it raises its wing covers slightly and rubs this scraper on the rough base of the wing cover. This sound may be heard for quite a distance. The wing covers of the male are longer than those of the female, and it is the male which produces the sound which we hear in the evenings. The female may also be distinguished from the male by the long sword-like ovipositor which extends from the rear end of her abdomen. This ovipositor is used to deposit the eggs, which she lays. in the ground. The eggs are generally deposited in the ground under a stone, but may be deposited other places where she is assurd they will be kept warm by the sun.

The head of the cricket is not so brilliantly marked as the head of the grasshopper. This is largely due to the dark color, and the fact that the eyes are not conspicuous. The cricket also has ears which can easily be seen as small white spots near the knee of the front leg. Both the male and female have long prongs or sword-like appendages which extend from the rear of the abdomen. In the case of the female, they are on each side of the ovipositor.

The cricket generally sings its song in the evening of late summer. The song or chirp may be a hostile war challenge to another male which may be near, it may be what seems to be a melancholy solo to relieve its own loneliness, or it may be a love song to attract its mate. If another male hears this war challenge, it will probably accept battle and a terrific struggle may follow in which one or both of the crickets may be severely injured.

The home of the cricket is to be found on the sunny side of the hill under a stone or protecting log. It is a great friend of the sun and is not very active unless the weather is warm. When the evening gets cool, it will cease to sing. Even the rapidity of the cricket's chirps seems to be dependent on the temperature. If the evening is very warm, it will chirp more rapidly than when it is colder. So accurately does it respond to the temperature of the air, that we can approximately determine the thermometer reading by using the following method:

Count the number of times the cricket chirps for one minute, divide this number by four, and add forty to the quotient. The result should be approximately the temperature as indicated by the thermometer.

The food of the cricket is grass and other forms of vegetation. It is not, however, so destructive as the grasshopper. This may be because the crickets do not appear in such large numbers nor are they able to move about so easily, having no wings.

QUESTIONS

1. Name four important parts of the cricket and give the purpose of each.

2. What sounds may the cricket make and when are they made?

3. What is an ovipositor?

4. How does the cricket produce sound?

5. What does the cricket eat?

6. What are palpi?

7. Where does the cricket live?

LESSON XIV

THE GREAT BATTLE AMONG PLANTS

There is a great battle going on among plants and trees continually. They do not use guns nor clubs in this warfare, but they kill each other just as certainly as if they used weapons.

If one goes to the forest where large trees are growing close together, he can readily see that the grass, weeds, and small shrubs cannot be found. What has become of them? Did they never grow here?

Every plant and tree must have soil, moisture, and sunlight if it is to live. Long ago, when the forest trees were very small bushes or plants, there were grass, shrubs, and weeds growing with

them. As these plants became larger their roots
began to struggle for the nourishment in the
ground and their tops began to struggle just as
fiercely for the sunlight by attempting to shade
each other.

The plants whose roots could grow most rapidly were able to get most of the plant food out
of the ground or soil. The other roots were
crowded out. Because these roots grew faster
than the others, they were able to push their
branches up into the air and sunlight more rapidly than the others and they could then get more
nourishment from the air. The plants that suc-
ceeded in doing this most easily were the young
trees. As soon as the trees had crowded out the
other plants so that they died, these trees began a
battle with each other. Those that could grow
the tallest were the ones that lived. Any tree that
could get its top and leaves above the other and
thus get the sunlight was the one that was allowed to live. Even the branches of the tall trees
that grew out from the trunk of the tree, but so
far down that they could not get the sunlight, died
and dropped off. So, after many years, we find
in the forest nothing but tall trees with very few
branches low down on the trunk.

In our vegetable gardens this same struggle is
going on. The plants are battling for moisture,

soil, and sunlight. If the weeds are allowed to get well started, their roots and branches will crowd out the vegetables we have planted.

It is very important that all weeds are kept out of the garden from the very first planting. If we try to remove the weeds after they have become well grown we will probably tear the roots of the vegetables. If the roots of the weeds are not all removed, but are broken off, the parts that remain in the ground will grow again.

QUESTIONS

1. Why is no grass found in a dense forest?

2. What three things are necessary for good plant growth?

3. For what are the plants continually struggling?

4. Why do some plants live while others die?

5. Why did not the grass or weeds crowd out the young trees instead of the trees crowding out the grass and weeds?

6. Why do the trees of the forest not have branches low down on the trunk?

7. How does this struggle occur in the vegetable garden?

8. When should the weeds be removed? Why?

9. Why is it more difficult to keep a garden free from weeds after the weeds get well started?

LESSON XV

ASPARAGUS

Asparagus requires a fertile soil t h a t has been well fertilized with w e l l rotted s t a b l e ma-nure. T h i s vegetable may b e produced f r o m seed, but it is much better to start with r o o t s that are one or two years old. T h e s e

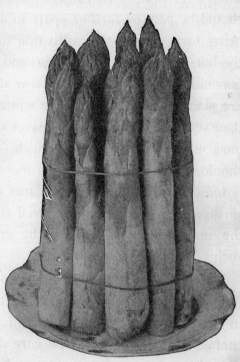

roots may be secured from dealers at a moderate price.

Asparagus will not grow well on wet ground or ground that is swampy. If the ground is nat-urally wet, it may produce good plants if drained.

If seed is used it should be planted in rows. When it is large enough to handle, it should be transplanted in rows at a distance of from one foot to one and one-half feet apart each way. If a horse is to be used for cultivation, these plants should be planted farther apart to avoid the roots being torn out by the cultivator or trampled by the horse. If roots are used instead of seeds, they may either be planted in the fall or spring. If they are planted in the fall and the winter is very cold, they should be covered with leaves or straw. Manure may be used for this mulch. The covering should not be more than three inches deep. If it is too deep, or is left on the plants too late in the spring, the roots will not get well started, because the sun cannot easily warm the ground through such a heavy mulch.

When the young asparagus sprouts are about five inches long above the ground, they are ready to cut. This is done by cutting off just below the surface of the ground. Great care should be taken that the crown or roots are not injured by this cutting.

All of the sprouts must be cut off when they reach the proper height or length. If a few are allowed to grow and mature, no more sprouts will grow from the same plant during the season. No sprouts should be cut the first season if the asparagus is started from seed. During the second season, and every season after the first, the sprouts should be cut until they become dry and tough from the hot, dry summer.

Late in the fall, when the vegetable tops have become dead, they should be cut off and placed in the compost heap. Care must be taken that weeds are not placed in this compost heap. All weeds that grow should be burned. If these weeds with their seed find their way to the compost heap, these weed seeds will find their way back to the garden in the fertilizer and will probably grow again.

After the garden has been thoroughly cleaned of all weeds and vegetable tops in the fall, all vegetable roots that are to remain in the ground during the winter should be well covered with about three inches of leaves, straw, or manure.

If manure can be obtained it is much better to use it, as it will not only protect as well as the leaves or straw, but it is a much better fertilizer for the following year's crop.

QUESTIONS

1. What kind of soil is necessary for asparagus?
2. In what two ways may this plant be started?
3. How should asparagus be transplanted?
4. When should asparagus be planted?

5. When should the asparagus be cut and how should it be cut?

6. Why should all of the sprouts be cut?

7. Why should the sprouts of asparagus that have been started from seed not be cut during the first season?

8. How should the garden be cleaned in late fall?

9. Why should weeds not be placed in the compost heap?

10. What protection should be given the roots that are to remain in the ground during the winter?

LESSON XVI

LETTUCE

Lettuce does not grow well in the hot sun. Because of this, the best lettuce is produced in the early spring or 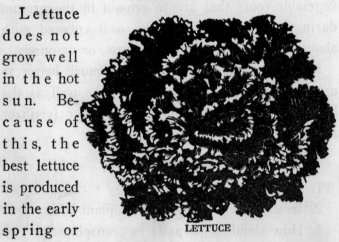 in the fall when the sun is not so warm. In order

LETTUCE

to produce early lettuce, the seed must
in a hotbed and the plants transplante
weather grows warmer.

The soil needed to produce good l
same as that required for asparagus,
there should be more sand in the soil.
loam in which there is much humus is well
for lettuce.

The seed should not be planted or sown mc
than one-half inch deep, so that it may get the
heat of the sun quickly. Lettuce should not be
used after it begins to flower, as it is then poisonous.

When the plants are transplanted they should
be placed about six inches apart in the rows, and
the rows should be from twelve to fifteen inches
apart.

Lettuce which grows rapidly is more tender
than that which grows slowly. If the ground is
rich and does not get too dry nor the sun too hot
the plants should grow quickly and be of good
quality. A board or screen may be arranged to
protect the plants during the hot hours of the day.

When the plants from the hotbed are transplanted to the garden, lettuce seed may also be
sown in the garden. This plan will bring a new

uce to maturity when the first crop has
This successive planting may be con-
hout the summer. Lettuce is one of
rtant greens.

QUESTIONS

n does lettuce grow best? Why?

w may early lettuce be produced?

ow deep should lettuce seed be planted?
Why?

4. Explain how lettuce should be transplanted.

5. When should lettuce be eaten? Why?

6. How should lettuce be grown to be of the best quality?

7. How may lettuce be protected from the hot sun?

8. What is meant by successive planting?

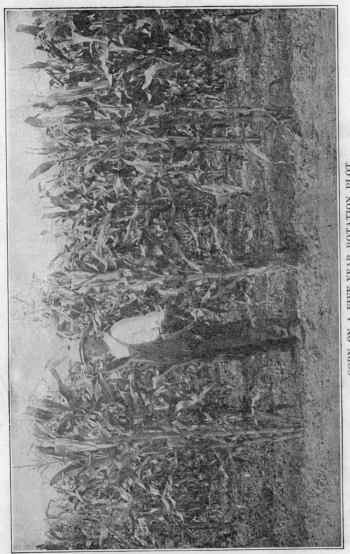

CORN ON A FIVE-YEAR ROTATION PLOT

LESSON XVII.

CORN

Corn is sometimes known as Indian corn or maize. The Indians are supposed to have been the first people who used it as food. Columbus took some of it to Spain when he returned from his explorations in America. In Canada the season is too short for corn to develop before frost. It is grown there for ensilage and to use green on the table. In some sections an early variety will mature.

Corn is one of the most important products of the United States. It is grown not only for use in the garden, as sweet corn is grown, but the common yellow variety is grown in fields sometimes containing hundreds of acres. This Indian corn or yellow corn is grown largely as food for cattle, horses, and hogs. Some of this corn is ground by mills into meal, from which bread, mush, and other kinds of food are made. Yellow corn forms one of the most important foods used for fattening hogs for market.

The stalks on which the corn grows are used in many sections of the country as food for cattle during the cold months of winter. These stalks when cut green are called fodder. Sometimes these stalks are cut into small pieces by machines and placed in a silo, or large tank. From this silo it is fed to cattle during the winter when there is no grass or pasture. When fed in this form it is called ensilage.

The time for planting corn varies in different parts of the country. The Indians planted it when the young oak leaves were as large as a squirrel's ears. The blossoming of the dogwood tree also told them it was time to plant corn.

The sweet corn of the garden is a particular kind of corn and may be bought in the market under different names. It should be planted in the garden in a square plot and not in one long row. The reason for this is that the pollen from the tassel or corn blossom must fall on the silk of the growing ears of corn, or the grains of corn will not develop. The pollen which comes from the tassel is the same kind of material which comes from the stamens of any flower. The silk of the corn is the pistils of the flower, and the pollen of flowers must fall on the pistils before the flower can be fertilized and produce seed.

Any rich ground will produce good corn, but some commercial fertilizer should be used. This fertilizer should be scattered over the soil before the corn is planted and mixed with the soil by using a rake or a harrow.

SHOCK OF FODDER AND PILE OF CORN HUSKED FROM IT

The corn should be planted in rows from two to three feet apart, depending on whether the corn is a short or tall variety. In these rows the corn may either be planted in hills, with five grains in a hill, two feet apart, or one grain in a place six inches apart. This seed should be covered with about two inches of soil.

When the corn has grown to about one inch above the ground it should be hoed or cultivated and all weeds removed. This cultivation should be repeated at least once each week until the corn has thoroughly shaded the ground. The corn should be cultivated after every rain as soon as the ground is sufficiently dry to work. This keeps the ground loose and pulverized so that the moisture cannot easily escape into the air.

Vining beans, or pole beans, may be planted close to the corn hills after the corn is about one foot high. The corn stalk will then serve as a pole on which the bean vine may climb.

When the corn is from four to six weeks old it should be thinned out. If the corn is not thinned there may be more ears of corn, but they will be small and imperfect. There will be more bushels of corn if the plants are thinned just as there will be more bushels of good apples if the apples are

GOLDEN BANTAM CORN—Splendid for table use

thinned at the proper time. The proper time is when they begin to use much of the nourishment of the tree or stalk. Corn cannot be transplanted.

Corn may be planted at different times to produce successive crops. This will make it possible to have fresh corn for the table during most of the summer.

Corn may be dried or canned for winter use with very little work or expense. The remaining corn from the garden, that is not used for the table, may be harvested and used for cattle or chickens.

QUESTIONS

1. What is corn sometimes called?
2. Why is it so called?
3. Name two varieties and state the use of each.
4. What use is made of the stalks of corn?
5. When should corn be planted?
6. Name two varieties of sweet corn.
7. Why should corn not be planted in one long row?
8. Explain how corn should be planted. Why should corn be planted in this way?
9. What is the purpose of cultivating corn?
10. How may beans be planted with corn? Why?
11. Why should corn be thinned?

LESSON XVIII

THE BEAN

The bean is supposed to be a native of regions near the Caspian Sea and in Egypt. Some of the ancient people did not know that the bean could be used for food and the priests at Rome were not allowed to eat it. These were the priests of Jupiter who held their positions during the early history of Rome.

Beans are produced best in a sandy loam soil. They will grow in almost any soil, but the largest crops are produced when there is considerable sand in the soil. Lima beans require a much richer soil than those of any other variety.

Beans may be produced within two months after planting. Several plantings should be made during the summer in order that they may mature at different times.

Beans are of two kinds, the climbing beans and the dwarf or bunch beans. The climbing beans require some sort of support. If poles are used as supports, they should be placed about one foot in the ground near the hill, but not near enough to tear the roots of the plant. The tops of four of these poles may be brought together and tied in order that the wind may not blow them over. Any support is good which keeps the vine up in the air where the sun may reach the leaves.

The dwarf beans do not need such rich soil as the climbing variety. Both kinds should be planted in rows from two to three feet apart, and in hills with five seeds to the hill, and about one foot apart in the row. When the seeds are planted the eye should be placed downward so that the root may be in its proper position and begin to grow quickly.

Beans cannot withstand frost, and if the plants are planted in the garden very early they may be killed by the frosts. If plantings are made one week apart, this loss by frost will not be serious unless a great quantity is planted.

More seeds should be planted in the hill than are wanted to grow. This will give an opportunity to thin out the imperfect plants and will also provide for some seeds that may not grow. Only three plants should be allowed to remain in each hill after thinning.

The seeds should not be covered to a depth of more than two inches and it should not be planted in the spring until the ground is warm.

The beans, while in the green pods, may be used for food or they may be canned with little

DWARF BUNCH BEANS

expense for winter use. The beans may be allowed to ripen and dry in the pods and then shelled and stored in a dry place for use during the winter.

Beans are sometimes made into flour. This flour is more nourishing than wheat flour and is sometimes used to adulterate wheat flour. Roasted beans are also sometimes used to adulterate coffee.

QUESTIONS

1. Where is the native land of the bean?
2. What kind of soil is best adapted for beans?
3. Why should several plantings of beans be made?
4. Name the two kinds of beans.
5. Explain how beans should be planted.
6. What is the purpose of poles when raising a crop of beans?
7. When may frost injure beans?
8. Explain how beans should be thinned and state why.
9. How should they be covered?
10. How may beans be preserved?
11. For what are beans sometimes used?

LESSON XIX

PEAS

Peas are produced in much the same way as beans. There are, however, a few differences which should be kept in mind. Supports or poles are not necessary except in the very tall varieties. Either clay or loam soil will produce a good crop of peas if manure has been placed on the ground during the previous year. It is not best to fertilize the ground during the year the peas are planted. A particular variety called sugar peas may be eaten with the green pods like beans.

The best method of planting peas varies somewhat from that of beans. Peas should be covered about one and one-half inches when planted, and then, as they grow, the soil should be raked in around the stalk until there is about four or five inches of soil above the pea which was planted. This will furnish additional nourishment for the plant and will also keep the plant from suffering from lack of moisture around the roots.

Peas should be planted in rows about two feet apart and in hills about one foot apart in the row. About four or five plants should grow in each hill.

PEAS

Peas are supposed to be native to southern Europe. Split peas are sometimes used for making soup and when ground are used for pudding. In the northern section of the United States and Canada, peas and pea vines are used to feed cattle. There is one variety called cowpeas, raisd largely in the south where they are used on the table.

QUESTIONS

1. Name two differences between beans and peas.

2. What is the native country of peas?

3. Explain how peas should be planted.

4. What kind of soil is best for peas?

5. For what are peas sometimes used?

LESSON XX

THE ONION

WHITE SILVERSKIN

Onions may be planted from seed or from sets. If sets are planted the onion will be ready to use much sooner than if the seed is planted. If, however, a large crop is to be pro-d u c e d, the seed should be planted, unless a considerable amount of money is to be expended on the crop, as the sets will cost much more than the seed.

Onions will grow in almost any kind of soil, but better onions may be grown on good soil.

Before the sets are planted the ground should be loose and well surface tilled. These sets should be planted in rows from six to eight inches apart, and the sets three inches apart in each row. They should not be covered more than one inch deep, but the soil should be well firmed down around the sets with the fingers. A board should not be used to firm the soil after planting because the sets may easily be injured. Care should be taken that the rows are straight. Straight rows of onions are much more easily cultivated than crooked ones. The onion bed, more than any other bed in the garden, gives the appearance of neatness if the rows are straight and all weeds are removed.

After the sets have sprouted, the ground between the rows should be cultivated with great care because the onions are easily torn loose from their place.

When the onions are about six inches high the soil should be raked in around the roots until it is about one inch deep about the stalk. This will keep the sun away from the lower part of the onion stalk and it will soon become as white and tender as the bulb from which the roots grow.

In three or four weeks from the time of planting, these onions will be ready to use. The larger ones should be used first and the smaller ones allowed to grow.

Before the onions begin to develop seed on the top of the stalks, they should be bent over by using a rake or board until the tops lie flat on the ground. This will keep much of the nourishment, which comes from the roots, in the bulb, and keep it from going up into the tops. This will cause the bulb to grow much larger. If this is not done the nourishment of the roots will go into the stalk to develop seed and the bulb will not be of so fine a quality.

If seed is planted, instead of sets, it should be sown in rows which are the same distance apart as those in which the sets are planted. When the young plants are large enough to handle they should be transplanted in the same way that sets are planted, except that they should be planted one-half inch deeper than the sets. Care should be used in transplanting these young onions that the roots are not torn and that the roots are not exposed to the sun during the process of transplanting. Successive crops of onions may be produced by planting seeds or sets about two weeks apart.

QUESTIONS

1. In what two ways may onions be planted?

2. What difference is there in the expense of seed and sets?

3. What kind of soil is best for onions?

4. How should onion sets be planted? How should onion seed be planted?

5. Why should onion rows be straight?

6. Why should the soil be raked in around the onion stalk after it has grown about six inches high?

7. How may the bulbs be made to grow larger after the onions have become almost mature?

8. What causes these bulbs to grow so much larger than they otherwise would grow?

9. What special care should be used when transplanting?

LESSON XXI

BEETS

Beets will grow in any rich soil that has a considerable quantity of lime in it. If the ground is swampy, it must be drained and limed. This lime may be scattered over the soil and raked in. The ground should be carefully surface tilled before the seeds are planted. All lumps of earth should be pulverized and the lime well mixed with the soil. This will not only aid in cultivating afterward but it will give the seeds a better chance to grow.

Before planting, examine the beet seeds carefully. If possible look at them under a magnifying glass. It will be seen that what seems to be one seed is, in reality, a cluster of little seeds. From each of these little seeds a plant will grow if the seed has not been injured.

BEET

The seeds should be planted in rows about ten inches apart, and about one inch apart in the row. These seeds should be covered with loose rich soil to the depth of about one inch. After planting, the soil should be firmed down with a board or other flat surface.

When the beets begin to show above the surface the ground should be cultivated and all weeds removed. Great care should be taken that the plants are neither uprooted nor covered during this cultivation.

When the plants can be handled they should be transplanted so that they may not crowd each other. In this transplanting they should be planted in rows ten inches apart, and four inches apart in the row. Only the largest and most vigorous plants should be transplanted. The plants not used in transplanting may be used as greens for food.

After the beets are transplanted, the ground should be carefully cultivated twice each week until the beet tops cover most of the ground. From this time on, the weeds should be removed but no cultivating done.

The beet root is the most important part of the plant used for food, but the tops are also used very much for greens, especially when the plants are young.

Several crops of beets may be produced if the seeds are planted at different times.

QUESTIONS

1. What kind of soil is best fitted for beets?

2. How may lime be added to the soil?

3. How should beets be planted?

4. What is the nature of beet seeds and what is their appearance?

5. Why should the soil be firmed down after the seeds are planted?

6. How often should beets be cultivated?

7. What parts of beets are used for food?

8. In what condition should the soil be before the seed is planted?

9. When should the cultivation of the soil cease when growing beets?

10. What care should be used in cultivation after transplanting?

LESSON XXII

RADISHES

Radishes are very well adapted to successive planting and may be planted with other vegetables that grow more slowly. They will then mature

and may be used before the other vegetables have developed. In order to have a good supply of young radishes, a supply may be planted each week. The radishes will be ready to use four weeks after they are planted if the soil is rich.

The soil best fitted for radishes is the same kind of soil best fitted for onions. Any rich

TURNIP RADISHES

loam soil will produce good radishes. Before planting, the soil should be well surface tilled and smooth.

Radishes are a native of temperate Asia. It is believed that more food may be grown on a certain plot of ground if radishes are planted than if any other vegetable is planted on the same area. This is partly due to the fact that radishes may be planted at any time during the entire summer. When some are removed for food, seed may be planted in their place.

Radishes, like lettuce, cannot easily endure the hot sun and may be produced with better results in the early spring or late summer. They should be grown as quickly as possible if they are to be of good quality.

Radishes are sometimes stored for winter in the garden. A hole is dug in the ground to a depth of about one foot. Dry straw is placed in the bottom of this pit and on this the radishes are placed. When the radishes are all in place and the tops have been removed, they are covered with a layer of dry straw. On this straw the earth is banked to a depth of a foot or more. Just so much earth should be placed on the radishes as will keep them from freezing.

Cabbage, turnips, beets, potatoes, and apples may be stored in the same way. Radishes may also be stored in the cellar.

QUESTIONS

1. How should the soil be prepared for planting radishes?

2. How should radish seed be planted?

3. How soon after planting may radishes be used?

4. During what season will radishes grow best? Why?

5. Explain in detail how radishes may be stored.

LESSON XXIII

CUCUMBERS

Cucumbers are a native of southern Asia and Egypt. It is mentioned by Vergil, the great Latin poet, as an article of food. Cucumbers were used as food in England during the early part of the fourteenth century.

Cucumbers require a very rich soil that has much humus in it. A generous quantity of commercial fertilizer should be used around the cucumber hills. This fertilizer should not be placed on the seed nor on the plants but should be so placed that the roots may easily reach it when they begin to grow. Well rotted stable manure may be used instead of commercial fertilizer. An excellent plan to follow is to dig a hole, where the hills are to be located, to the depth of about one foot. In this hole place about six inches of well rotted manure. On this place about two or three inches of good soil and on this soil plant the seed, which

CUCUMBERS

should be covered with about two inches of good soil. If neither manure nor commercial fertilizer is available, a generous quantity of well rotted material from the compost heap may be used instead.

As soon as the plants get well started, the roots will go down into this fertilizer and thus get the best supply of nourishment for the growing plant.

The ground must be well surface tilled before the seed is planted. The seed should be planted in rows four feet apart, and in hills three feet apart in the row.

The cucumber plant is a very popular plant among some insects, especially the flea-beetle and the cucumber beetle. Other insects, some that bite the leaves and some that suck the sap, injure the cucumber very much. When the plants are very young they should be sprayed with a solution of arsenate of lead in the proportion of one ounce to one gallon of water, or the arsenate of lead may be used in the powered form by dusting it on the leaves. This will kill all biting insects. The plants should be watched very carefully and if they should be attacked by insects that suck the sap, they should be sprayed by using the nicotine sulphate solution which is used to kill plant lice.

The cucumber forms an important product, both as a fresh food and for pickling purposes. They are eaten fresh as salad, or may be cooked like the egg plant.

QUESTIONS

1. Explain what kind of soil will produce cucumbers best.

2. What kind of fertilizer should be used?

3. Explain clearly how cucumbers should be planted.

4. Why should the fertilizer or manure be placed under the seed?

5. Name three insects which attack the cucumber.

6. How may these insects be killed?

7. For what kind of insects is arsenate of lead used?

8. How is the solution of arsenate of lead made?

9. For what kind of insects is the nicotine sulphate solution used?

10. How is the nicotine sulphate solution made?

LESSON XXIV

POTATOES

Irish potatoes require a rich loam soil with a considerable amount of potash in it. Deep cultivation is also necessary in order that a good crop may be produced.

The potato is a native of Chile and Peru. It was taken to Spain early in the sixteenth century. Sir

John Hawkins is supposed to have taken it to England about the year of 1565 from Virginia, to which colony it was taken by the Spanish explorers.

Soil that is poor or that does not have potash in it will not produce a good potato crop. When the ground has been well surface tilled and smoothed

IRISH COBBLER

it should be "furrowed out." This is done by plowing a furrow about five inches deep across the surfaced ground. These furrows should be straight, and three feet apart. In these furrows the seed should be planted. The potato sprouts grow from the "eye" of the potato. In preparing potatoes for planting, the seed potato may be cut into a number of parts, so that one or more "eyes" may be left undisturbed in a part, and these pieces planted. If the "eye" is uninjured the potato will grow. Several plants may be sprouted in different places from one potato, one or more pieces in a place, and one foot apart. The seed should then be covered to the depth of about three inches. As the plants grow, more soil should be raked around the plants until the soil in the row is level with the soil between the rows. The potato which was planted will then be from four to five inches deep, and better able to withstand the dry weather than if it were not planted so deep. The plants will thus be kept erect and there will be no danger of the sun burning the potatoes that might otherwise be exposed.

Potatoes should be cultivated once each week either by a horse cultivator or a hoe, and all weeds should be removed.

As soon as the tops begin to die the potatoes may be used. While the potatoes are being dug they should not be exposed to the sun but should be kept covered with burlap or straw until they are stored.

In order that potatoes may be kept with little danger from rotting or wilting, they must be kept in a dry place, a dark place, and at a temperature of about forty-two degrees Fahrenheit.

Insects injure potatoes very much while they are growing. During the cold winter months in the north, the potato beetle lives in the ground. When the weather becomes warm in the spring this insect comes out of his winter home and begins to look around for food. If it can find a young potato plant it will look no farther, because it likes potato plants very much.

This potato beetle looks something like a grain of coffee, with black and brown stripes running along its back. It injures the potato by biting and eating the leaves. Very soon after the beetle has found the potato plant, little clusters of yellow eggs may be seen on the leaves. In a few days black grubs will hatch from these eggs. These grubs grow very rapidly and eat great quantities of potato leaves. If these beetles and grubs are not killed very soon after they appear, there will be nothing left of the potato plant except the stalk.

When the grubs are mature they crawl into the ground and remain there for about two weeks. During these two weeks they have gone through the pupa stage and come out of the ground as beetles. These new beetles lay eggs and more

DIFFERENT STAGES OF THE POTATO SCAB

grubs are hatched. This process continues until late in the summer. The potato beetle is one injurious insect that is not relished by birds. Birds are great protectors of plant life, as they destroy insect pests in great numbers, but few birds will attack the potato beetle. The beautiful Rose-breasted

Grosbeak is not only elegant in appearance and song, but is a favorite bird among gardeners because, as an insect eater, it makes no distinction as to the pest it attacks, and it devours the potato beetle with the same relish as it does flies, wasps, and grubs. The Rose-breasted Grosbeak should be encouraged to visit the gardens, as many potato crops have been saved through its efforts.

A solution of arsenate of lead will destroy these beetles and grubs and all other insects that eat or bite the leaves. This solution should be applied by spraying once each week.

Potato scab may be avoided by washing the seed potatoes in solution of formaldehyde in the proportion of one-half pint of formaldehyde to twelve gallons of water.

Bordeaux mixture should be used for blight. Another potato disease which produced a famine in Ireland by the entire destruction of the potato crop during the years of 1845-1847, and in 1860 the destruction was almost as great, may be avoided by powdering the seed potatoes with flowers of sulphur before planting.

QUESTIONS

1. What particular thing must be in the soil to produce good potatoes?

2. How should the ground be furrowed out and the potatoes planted?

3. What is the purpose of planting the potatoes so deep as four or five inches?

4. How often should potatoes be cultivated?

5. When are the potatoes ready to use?

6. How should potatoes be stored?

7. Describe the potato beetle. Explain how it develops.

8. How may the potato beetle be destroyed? What bird will attack it?

9. What is the best remedy for potato scab?

10. How may potato blight be avoided?

11. How should the seed potatoes be prepared for planting?

LESSON XXV

THE POTATO BEETLE

Among the most common and most destructive insects which annoy farmers and gardeners is the potato beetle. This beetle is a native of America and, before potatoes were extensively grown in this country, fed on other vegetation and did little damage. Now it is one of the greatest pests of agricultural sections. The potato beetle seems to have been first located in Colorado and Arizona and, because of this, is sometimes called the Colorado potato beetle. It began to spread its destructiveness in the year 1858 and in ten years it had covered about one-fourth of the entire United States and Canada.

Many destructive insects are eaten by birds, and, because of this, their numbers do not become alarming. Only one bird, however, will eat potato beetles. This may be due to either their odor or taste. The Rose-breasted Grosbeak is the only bird that will eat the potato beetle.

The mature potato beetle is yellow in color, striped with black. It spends the winter in the ground where it can escape the cold weather. In the spring these beetles come out of the ground at about the time the potato plants begin to grow. The mother beetle lays her eggs on the underside of the leaves of the potato plants. In about eight days, small reddish-yellow larvae with small black dots on each side hatch from these eggs. The head of the larva is so drawn down on the under side toward the tail that it has a very peculiar and cramped appearance.

These larvae will eat very much during their growing period, or until they reach maturity, which requires about three weeks. During this time they will molt four times. When the larva has become full grown, it will go down to the ground and form a shell or covering about itself and change into a pupa. It remains in this stage for about ten days when it emerges a full grown beetle. It is now ready to lay more eggs from which other larvae will hatch. There are usually two generations of potato beetles each season, and from each female beetle there are from four hundred to five hundred larvae produced.

If the larvae or beetles are handled, they will secrete a bad smelling liquid which serves them as a good weapon of defense. It is probably because of this liquid that birds will not molest them. This may also be the cause of their fearlessness.

The mature beetle has compound eyes which are black in color and three simple eyes on the top of its head. Like most insects, it has three pairs of short legs on which are both claws and pads. It, however, does not depend on these short legs for traveling from one place to another. It is capable of flying with wings which it keeps protected under its striped wing covers. When it flies, it holds its wing covers forward rigidly in much the same way as the grasshopper. The potato beetle also has short antennae and two pairs of palpi around its mouth.

The remedy most generally used to destroy the potato beetle is the arsenate of lead solution. This solution will destroy anything which eats vegetation. This remedy should be applied with a spray just after the larvae have hatched from the eggs.

QUESTIONS

1. Where did the potato beetle originate?
2. Where does the potato beetle stay during the winter?
3. Describe the larvae.

4. How much time is required for the eggs to hatch?

5. What do the larvae do to escape their enemies?

6. How much time is required for the larvae to reach maturity?

7. Describe the mature beetle.

Q. How many larvae may one female produce in one season?

9. How may the potato beetle be destroyed?

10. What bird will eat the potato beetle?

LESSON XXVI

SPINACH

Spinach is used entirely as greens. It is one of the most important garden products. It is grown best in the northern sections of the United States and in Canada, because of the favorable conditions for rapid growth. For this reason it grows best in spring and fall. When the seeds begin to develop, the plant is too dry and tough for greens.

The soil best adapted for spinach is a rich dry loam which has been enriched with commercial fertilizer containing nitrate of soda. This fertilizer will furnish nitrogen for the plant. A sulphate of ammonia fertilizer may be used instead of the nitrate of soda.

The seeds should be planted in April or as soon as the ground can be cultivated. The rows in which the seeds are sown should be twelve inches apart. When planted, the seeds should be covered with an inch of loose soil. When the plants are about five or six inches high, one inch more soil should be raked in around the plants. The soil should be cultivated sufficiently to maintain a loose surface around the plants. This loose surface will keep the moisture from evaporating during the hot dry days.

If the weather remains hot and dry for a considerable period of time, the spinach must be watered if it is to remain tender and of good quality.

The leaves and head of the spinach are the only parts that are used for food. These leaves are large and require a great deal of moisture to keep them fresh and growing. During the hot, dry weeks of mid-summer, the ground does not have much moisture near the surface and the spinach plants will die if they are not watered.

This water should be applied in the evening in order that it may reach the roots before it is evaporated by the hot sun.

The spinach plant when harvested is cut off just under the surface of the ground.

QUESTIONS

1. What are greens?

2. Where does spinach grow best?

3. Why is spinach not good for food when the seeds begin to develop?

4. What kind of soil is best adapted for spinach?

5. What kind of fertilizer should be used for spinach?

6. When should spinach be planted?

7. How should it be planted?

8. What is the purpose of keeping the soil loose around the plants?

9. What part of the spinach is used for food?

10. When should plants be watered?

LESSON XXVII

TURNIPS

Turnips are regarded by many people as the hardiest crop produced in the garden and the crop that requires least care. Turnip seeds are some-times sown as a follow-up crop after other vegetables have been harvested. In some cases no particular care is used in sowing turnips except that the weeds are removed and the ground smoothed. The seeds are then sown broadcast and raked or harrowed in. From this method many turnips may

PURPLE-TOP GLOBE
TURNIPS

be produced, but the method of planting is careless and the result is not always satisfactory.

Any rich soil that is not too dry will produce good turnips. Some commercial fertilizer may be used but no stable manure. The seeds should be sown in rows, about one foot apart, and the seeds about two inches apart in the row. The seeds may be sown closer than two inches to provide for some that may not grow. After planting, the seeds should be covered with about one-half inch of soil, but it should not be firmed down.

After the plants appear above the surface of the ground, they should be thinned out, so that the plants will be about four inches apart. All weeds must be carefully removed and the ground thoroughly cultivated each week until the leaves cover most of the ground. At least two crops of turnips may be raised, one in the spring and the other in the fall.

The insects that attack turnips may be destroyed in the same manner as was suggested for cucumber pests. Turnips are, however, not so popular with insects as are cucumbers.

In Canada, and some of the northern states, large crops of turnips are raised for stock feed. The ruta-baga, or Swedish turnip, is closely allied to the white turnip which we eat, but is cultivated mostly for cattle.

QUESTIONS

1. What is meant by a follow-up crop?

2. How is turnip seed sometimes sown?

3. Why is this not the best method to use in sowing turnip seed?

4. Explain how turnip seed should be planted and thinned out.

5. What kind of soil is best for turnips?

6. How are the insects that injure turnips to be destroyed?

LESSON XXVIII

CABBAGE

Almost every garden has a "cabbage patch." Cabbage is served in so many ways and so commonly used that it is one of the most popular vegetables, and has become a very important product in many parts of the world.

Any rich soil will produce good cabbage. Cabbage should not be planted in the same place each year, because the soil is likely to become diseased from the decayed parts of the preceding crop if these were not removed from the garden.

The seeds should be planted in a hotbed about six weeks before they are to be transplanted to the garden. During the last week or ten days before they are transplanted to the garden, they should be exposed to the air at all times when the weather is not too cold. This will strengthen the plants so that when they are transplanted they will be able to endure a late frost without injury.

Great care should be used in this transplanting. The plants have large leaves and a great amount

CABBAGE

of water is evaporated from them while they are exposed to the sun. If these plants are transplanted from the hotbed to the garden in the morning of a hot day, they will probably die before evening. The sun evaporates more moisture from the leaves than the roots can supply, because the roots have not yet become properly connected with the soil in their new home. The plants should be transplanted in the evening and protected from the sun by a shade or screen for one or two days. The roots will then be able to secure nourishment and moisture from the ground. In this way the plants will not be injured.

Cabbage does not grow well in the hot weeks of summer and should be grown in the spring and late summer.

When transplanted, the plants should be placed in rows three feet apart, and one and one-half feet apart in the row. These plants should be transplanted when the ground is not too dry.

Wood ashes should be used as a fertilizer near the roots of each plant. If ashes cannot be obtained, lime may be used instead. This will not only fertilize the plants but will sterilize the ground and lessen the danger from such diseases as club-root, which frequently attack cabbage plants. The soil should be cultivated frequently that it may be kept loose and pulverized.

QUESTIONS

1. Why should cabbage not be planted in the same place from year to year?

2. How should plants become accustomed to the weather before they are transplanted? Why?

3. What special care should be taken when transplanting cabbage plants?

4. When should plants be transplanted? Why?

5. How should cabbage plants be planted in the garden?

6. What kind of fertilizer should be placed around the plants? Why?

7. During what time of year do cabbage plants grow best?

LESSON XXIX

CARROTS

Carrots are much like turnips, radishes, or parsnips. The part of each of these plants that is used for food grows under the ground; they look

CARROTS

much alike, and are nearly the same shape. Carrots may be grown on any garden soil if commercial fertilizer is used. When the ground has become warm and sufficiently dry to work easily, it should be spaded or plowed to a depth of five or six inches. It should then be well surface tilled and the ground made smooth. While the ground is being surface tilled, the commercial fertilizer should be scattered on the ground and raked in. The rows should then be marked out about one inch deep, and from ten to twelve inches apart. In these rows the carrot seeds should be sown. It is easy to make a mistake by sowing too many seeds, because they are very small. To avoid this mistake, the seeds may be thoroughly mixed with dry sand before they are sown. If this is done, there will not be so much danger of getting the seeds too thick. After the seeds are sown they should be covered with about one-half inch of soil, which should be firmed down. The plants should be thinned out when about two inches high, to about two inches apart. The ground should be thoroughly cultivated once each week until the leaves shade the ground. There are several kinds of carrots. Some are adapted to spring planting and some to late summer planting. Seed catalogs will give information concerning the time for planting each variety.

Carrots may be stored in a garden pit or in the cellar. If stored in the cellar, they should be put in a dark, dry place where there is good ventilation and a temperature of from forty to forty-five degrees.

Carrots are also used as feed for cattle, and some attempts have been made to make sugar from them.

CARROTS

When grown for table use, they should be harvested before they blossom or they will become woody and tough. The plant will grow to a height of about two feet before it produces these flowers, which are white in color.

QUESTIONS

1. Name three garden vegetables which are much like carrots.

2. When should carrots be planted?

3. How should the ground be prepared for the planting of carrots?

4. How should the seeds be planted?

5. Explain how carrots may be stored.

6. When should they be harvested? Why?

7. How tall do carrots grow?

LESSON XXX

PARSNIPS

Parsnips, in some particulars, are different from all other vegetables. They require a deeper soil; their seeds are more easily injured, and they can remain in the ground where they grow during the entire winter. The soil best adapted to parsnips is a loose, rich soil. The roots grow deep into the ground and because of this, the ground must be spaded or plowed to a depth of at least one foot.

When the long tap root begins to push its way down into the soil, it will have much less difficulty in finding its way if the ground is loose.

After the ground is spaded, it should be surface tilled in much the same way as the ground was prepared for carrots. Commercial fertilizer should also be raked into the soil before the seed is planted.

When the ground is well surfaced and smooth, it should be marked out in rows one foot apart, and one inch deep. In this furrow, which is one inch deep, the seeds should be planted. If the seeds have been tested by sprouting, and they are found to be fifty per cent good, there should be about three of these seeds planted to the inch. If the test shows only one seed out of every four to be good, then there should be more than three planted to the inch. After the seeds are planted there should be one-half inch of soil placed on the seeds and firmed down.

As soon as the parsnips have reached the height of two inches they should be thinned to two inches apart. The ground should be kept thoroughly free from weeds and the surface kept loose until the plants have developed a good shade.

The parsnips that are to be used for food should be harvested before they develop seeds. Plants that have grown from seeds that have been planted late in the summer will probably not develop seeds before the winter stops their growth.

Parsnips may be stored in a garden pit or placed in a damp cellar and covered with sand. Those that are to be left in the ground where they have grown, should be covered when the weather begins to get cold. This covering should be straw or leaves and should be about four inches deep. Some soil may be thrown on the straw or leaves to keep the wind from blowing the covering away. When the danger of freezing is over in the spring, this covering should be removed and the parsnips taken out of the ground.

QUESTIONS

1. In what ways are parsnips different from other vegetables?

2. How should the ground be prepared for parsnips? Why?

3. How should the ground be marked out for planting parsnips?

4. How should parsnips be planted?

5. How may parsnips be stored?

6. How should those that are left in the ground all winter be cared for?

7. How deep do parsnips grow?

LESSON XXXI

SWISS CHARD

Swiss chard is an excellent vegetable to be used as greens. The ground must be well limed to produce good plants, especially if the ground has not been well drained.

The ground should be plowed or spaded to a depth of six inches and well surface tilled. While the ground is being surface tilled, some commercial fertilizer should be raked in with the soil.

The rows should be marked out twelve inches apart and the furrows one to one and one-half inches deep. About two seeds should be planted to the inch and covered one inch deep with good soil. When the plants are sufficiently large to handle, they should be thinned to about five or six inches apart. The plants that are removed may easily be transplanted if desired. Only the most vigorous should be left to grow.

If possible, examine the seeds of the Swiss chard under a magnifying glass before they are planted. Will each of the seeds produce one or more plants?

The cultivation of these plants should be thoroughly done each week and no weeds should be permitted to start.

The leaves are the most important part of the vegetable and should be cut off from the outside only. If the inner leaves are cut the plant will either die or become dwarfed, because it will not have sufficient leaf surface to furnish nourishment for its growth. The stalks may also be used as greens if they are used before the plant becomes too old.

QUESTIONS

1. How should the ground be prepared for Swiss chard?

2. How should the ground be marked out?

3. How should the seed be planted?

4. How should the plants be thinned?

5. How should the leaves be cut when they are ready for use?

6. Of what use are the stalks?

LESSON XXXII

KOHL-RABI

Kohl-rabi is a sort of second cousin to the cabbage. It is not nearly so common as the cabbage and is not so well known. It is grown best in good rich soil and under soil conditions much like those which make the cabbage thrive best.

The ground should be prepared in the same way as for Swiss chard. The rows should be furrowed out twelve inches apart and one inch deep and after the seeds are planted the soil should be firmed down. Two seeds should be sown to the inch.

When the plants are about two or three inches tall, they should be thinned to five inches apart. Cultivate or rake the soil between the rows frequently. All weeds must be kept removed.

The part of the kohl-rabi that is used for food is the part of the stalk just above the ground, which becomes very much enlarged as the plant grows. In about two weeks after the plant comes above the ground the lower part of the stalk begins to swell and will finally become more than two inches thick. It is this thick part that is prepared for food and should be used before the plant becomes too old. When the plant becomes mature, this enlarged part

KOHL-RABI

of the stalk becomes tough in much the same way that radishes become tough and woody.

Kohl-rabi should be planted as early in the spring as the ground can be tilled, because it grows better in the spring or fall than in the hot weeks of summer.

The seeds may be planted at several different times and in this way tender plants will always be ready for use.

When the plants are harvested, no part of the plant should be used except this enlarged part of the stalk. Great care should be taken while cultivating that the soil is not raked against this enlarged part.

Kohl-rabi, like cabbage, is attacked by insects. Sometimes plant lice attack it. These pests may easily be destroyed by using the arsenate of lead solution for insects that bite the leaves and the nicotine sulphate solution for the plant lice. These pests should never be allowed to get started on the plants.

QUESTIONS

1. In what ways is kohl-rabi like cabbage?

2. How should the seeds be planted, and how should the plants be thinned?

3. What part of the plant is used as food?

4. When should kohl-rabi be planted?

LESSON XXXIII

GARDEN PROTECTORS

Very few people realize what would happen to all vegetable gardens if there were no wild life. It is true that rabbits may eat much of the cabbage and lettuce, rats and crows may eat some of the corn, and birds may eat many of the berries and cherries, but birds and wild animals, in most cases, pay well for the damage they do.

The toad is a most valuable protector of the garden, because his food is almost entirely made up of insects that are harmful. The toad is a very humble helper and should never be driven away nor killed. Snakes are his worst enemies and he should be protected from them. It has been estimated that a toad is worth $19.00 to a gardener.

Birds are mostly responsible for keeping insect life so reduced that we may grow our vegetables without having them destroyed by insects. Birds frequent vegetable gardens and flower gardens to secure bugs and insects for their own food and for their young. Birds have been known to take into their mouths at one time, from the garden, more than one hundred harmful insects. These they used as food. Birds should be encouraged to nest in the garden or near it so that they may aid in keeping it free from pests.

Cats and birds will not get on well together in the same garden. The birds will either be killed by the cat, or they will leave for other localities. Even cats that have good reputations for decency, will kill birds when food is wanted and sometimes they will even kill them when they are not hungry. These cats are often found out in the fields still-hunting for birds. These house cats do not go out in pairs, but alone. No animal that hunts alone may be thoroughly domesticated. The cat may be useful for destroying rats and mice, but the birds will save us more than the rats and the mice destroy and the rats and mice may easily be destroyed without the cat.

Bird boxes that are adapted to the birds of the locality should be erected in the garden in suitable places. Bird baths should be erected, but not closer to the ground than eight feet, and a few bread crumbs should be scattered in the garden each morning. With such kindness the birds will soon feel at home in the garden. They will not only protect the garden from many harmful insects, but they will add their song to the joyousness of the home and its surroundings.

1. Name some animals that injure the garden.

2. Do these aid the garden in any way?

3. What forms of life aid the garden most?

4. Why may not cats and birds live in the garden together?

5. Can cats be trained not to kill birds?

LESSON XXXIV

THE EARTH

The earth is a large body which, in shape, is almost as round as an orange. It is, however, flattened somewhat at the poles. When we see high mountains and deep valleys, it is sometimes difficult for us to think that the earth is round. These deep valleys and high mountains, however, have about the same effect on the shape of the earth as the small ridges on the outside of the orange. These ridges are too small to affect, in any noticeable degree, the shape of the orange, so the valleys and mountains are too small, compared with the size of the earth, to affect its shape very much.

The earth is only one of the spheres which exist in the universe, and it is one of the smallest. The universe includes all space in which are many bodies such as the earth. Many of these heavenly bodies are so far away that it is impossible to see them. Many of them can only be seen with the aid of a very powerful telescope. The "Milky Way," which seems like a band of mist or white clouds stretched across the sky, is, in reality, made up of a very great number of stars. This "Milky Way" is sometimes called "Jacob's Ladder."

The poles of the earth are the two points through which the axis of the earth passes. On this axis the earth rotates, or turns, as it moves through space around the sun. It requires twenty-four hours for the earth to rotate once on its axis.

The earth, in addition to rotating on its axis, revolves around the sun. It requires one year for the earth to revolve once around the sun. Since the circumference of the earth is about 25,000 miles, and it rotates once every twenty-four hours, a point on the equator must travel very rapidly in order to travel so many miles in one day.

While the earth is rotating on its axis, that side of the earth on which we live is turned toward the sun part of the time and away from the sun part of the time. When it is turned away from the sun, we have night; and when it is turned toward the sun, we have daylight. In the summer this daylight period is longer than in the winter because the sun is shining more directly on the northern part of the earth.

The revolution of the earth is the cause of our seasons. During the winter the northern part of the earth on which we live is turned slightly away from the sun and remains in this position until spring, although the earth keeps rotating and revolving continually.

The earth is called a planet because it revolves around the sun. The sun has seven other planets besides the earth. Of these planets, Mercury and Venus are nearer the sun than the earth.

Some of the planets have smaller bodies, called satellites or moons, revolving around them. The earth has one moon. The sun with its eight planets and their moons is called the solar system, the sun being the center. The moon requires one month to revolve around the earth. It gives out no light of its own but reflects the light which comes to it from the sun, just as a reflector will reflect the light in our homes.

The moon is about 250,000 miles from the earth. The earth is about 93,000,000 miles from the sun. The sun is much larger than the earth, and the earth is much larger than the moon. Let us suppose that a large ball about two feet in diameter represents the sun, and about two hundred feet from this large ball an ordinary garden pea represents the earth, and about six inches from this pea is a grain of No. 6 shot which represents the moon. This will give us a fair idea of the relative sizes and distances of the sun, earth and moon.

Before Columbus came from Spain to the western continent, many people thought the earth was flat like a table and that if one traveled too far, he would come to the edge and either drop off or be devoured by great sea monsters or evil spirits of some kind. Since that time, men have come to know much about the earth and heavenly bodies. We now know the earth is round because men have traveled around it; because when a ship comes in from sea we see the top first, and because when the earth comes between the sun and the moon and partly shuts off the light as it shines against the moon, we see the shadow of the earth on the moon; this shadow is circular or in the form of a crescent.

QUESTIONS

1. What is the shape of the earth?

2. What is meant by the poles of the earth?

3. What is meant by the earth's axis.

4. What is meant by rotation and revolution?

5. How long does it take the earth to rotate once and revolve once?

6. What causes night?

7. What is a planet? What is a satellite? What is a solar system?

8. How far is the earth from the sun? How far is the moon from the earth?

9. Name the earth, moon, and sun in the order of size.

10. What was once the opinion of men concerning the shape of the earth?

11. How do we know the earth is round?

LESSON XXXV

STARS

Stars are large heavenly bodies, some of which may even be larger than our sun. The "Milky Way" is thought to be made up of suns, each of which may have planets revolving around it in much the same way as the planets revolve around our sun. Whether or not these stars which compose the "Milky Way" are suns, they are almost without number, and their light is so blended that it appears as a white cloud instead of light which comes from stars. An observer, when looking through a large telescope at the "Milky Way," estimated that 240,000 stars passed the observed spot in the heavens in forty-one minutes.

These stars are all moving very rapidly through space, probably around a common center. They may be moving millions of miles per day, and yet, because of their great distance from us, may not seem to be moving at all. When we consider that the earth is only one of the smallest of eight planets revolving around the sun, and that each shining star is probably another sun around which many other planets are revolving, we must recognize that the earth is a very small part of the universe.

A constellation is a group of stars. One of the most prominent of the constellations of the heavens is called Ursa Major, the Big Dipper being a part of this constellation. This Big Dipper is made up of seven stars. The last two stars of the bowl of the dipper point toward the Pole Star. This Pole Star is the first star in the handle of another dipper called the Little Dipper. These stars may be seen in the heavens toward the north during the entire year.

Orion is another constellation found in the southern heavens during the evenings of February. It is composed of three bright stars which represent Orion's belt, and a curved line of smaller stars below the three brighter ones, representing his sword. This constellation is probably the most conspicuous in the southern heavens.

Sirius, the Great Dog Star in literature, was supposed by the ancients to be one of the two dogs which followed the great hunter Orion. It is located in a direct line with the three stars composing the belt of Orion, and on the curved side of the sword. Above Sirius is located Procyen, the Little Dog Star, and at a little greater distance from Orion than Sirius.

Cassiopeia's Chair is another constellation which is always above the horizon in the latitude of New

York. It is found on the opposite side of the Pole Star from the Great Dipper. It is made up of five brilliant stars which form the W-shaped chair, the top part of the W being turned toward the Pole Star.

The Dragon is a constellation located between the Big Dipper and the Pole Star. The tail of the Dragon is between the bowl of the Dipper and the Pole Star. Twelve stars make up this constellation, four of which compose the head.

QUESTIONS

1. What is the nature of a star?
2. What is the "Milky Way"?
3. What is a constellation? Name three.
4. Describe the constellation which is most prominent in the southern heavens. When may this constellation be seen?
5. Where is the Big Dipper located?
6. What is the Pole Star and where is it located?
7. How may the Little Dipper be found?
8. Where is the Dragon and how many stars are contained in it?
9. How may Sirius be found?
10. Describe and locate Cassiopeia's Chair.

LESSON XXXVI

CURRENTS

Currents may be formed in the water or in the air. Currents in the water may easily be seen in a small stream where the water flows around a curve in its course. Some of the water may be flowing very rapidly and some may be almost stationary. This is caused by the force of the water as it flows around the curve on its way down the stream.

In the ocean there are many currents flowing through the water in much the same way as water flows through the land. This is not caused by the force of the water flowing down hill as in the case of a small stream, but by the rotation of the earth and by the temperature of the water.

Most substances are light when their temperature is high and heavy when their temperature is low. Air, when it is warm, will rise. This may easily be noticed from the strong upward movement of the air over a bonfire. This current of air is sometimes so strong that it will carry small pieces of burnt weed high into the air. The cold air in the room of the homes where we live is found near the floor and the warm air near the ceiling. This is so because the cold air is heavy and the warm air is light.

Clouds may come very close to the surface of the earth at night because they become cold and heavy, and rise again as soon as the sun warms them the following day. These clouds are sometimes called fog, when they are close to the earth. These clouds rise very slowly and descend very slowly. When the air becomes warm and rises, the air which is cold rushes in to take its place. This constant movement of the air is called wind. Sometimes this movement is so strong that it may destroy buildings and uproot trees.

Wherever the surface of the earth is being heated by the sun, this movement of the air is taking place. The wind always blows toward the place which is heated. At this heated area the air rises because it is warm and light. When this air rises to some distance from the earth, it becomes cool and heavy, and again begins to fall toward the earth.

There are many different kinds of winds. Some receive their names from the rapidity of their movements, some from their direction, and some from their location. Cyclones, hurricanes, monsoons, whirlwinds, and land and sea breezes are some of the names given to winds or air currents.

Currents of water flow through the ocean in much the same way that currents of air move around through our atmosphere. The cause for these water currents is, in general, the same as for the air currents.

The rotation of the earth is another cause for the movements of the air and for ocean currents. The earth requires twenty-four hours to rotate once on its axis. The circumference of the earth at the equator is about twenty-five thousand miles. In order that a point on the equator may move around the earth in twenty-four hours, it must travel at the rate of more than a thousand miles per hour. Since the air is not a fixed part of the earth, as are the trees, it does not move at the same rate as the earth. The result is that when the earth whirls around at this terrific rate, the air near the surface seems to rush or blow in the opposite direction.

Water, like air, will expand and get light when it is warmed, and will rise to the surface of the ocean or stream. Should the water at the surface become cold, it will then sink to the bottom. Water is a very peculiar substance in one particular. It will become light above 39.2 degrees Fahrenheit and it will also become light when it gets colder than 39.2 degrees. At this particular temperature of 39.2 degrees Fahrenheit or 4 degrees Centigrade, it is heaviest. All of the water at the bottom of the ocean must be at this temperature for the reason that some of the ocean water is much colder than this temperature and some of it is much warmer. Frozen water is lighter than water at 39.2 degrees and will float on the surface.

These water currents may be caused by the rotation of the earth or by the different temperatures of the water, just as those two causes produce currents in the air. These water currents generally flow from the equator, partly because the water is warmest at this point, and partly because the movement of the earth is greatest at this point. The Gulf Stream flows north from the equator in the Atlantic ocean, and the Japan current flows north from the equator in the Pacific ocean. The names applied to these currents are generally taken from some body of water or from some country near where the current starts. There are a great many ocean currents in the water area of the earth. These water currents are very valuable because they aid commerce and temper the climate of the countries near their course. The climate of England is much warmer than it otherwise would be if the warm Gulf Stream did not strike its coast. The climate of California is adapted to the production of tropical fruits because the Japan current warms its shores.

QUESTIONS

1. Name two kinds of currents.

2. What effect does temperature have on the weight of many substances?

3. Will warm air in a room remain near the floor or near the ceiling? Why?

4. What causes air currents and water currents?

5. How strong may air currents become?

6. What is fog?

7. What determines the direction of the wind?

8. Name four kinds of winds. What determines the different kinds?

9. Name two important ocean currents. In what direction do they flow? Why?

10. What is the circumference of the earth at the equator? How long does it require the earth to rotate once on its axis?

11. How does the rotation affect the movement of the air or water?

THE MUSKRAT

12. How fast does a point on the surface of the earth at the equator move as the earth rotates?

13. How do ocean currents receive their names?

14. Of what value are ocean currents?

15. Name two places that are benefited by ocean currents.

LESSON XXXVII.

RAIN

No country can be productive without rain. The Sahara desert is barren because little or no rain falls on it. Many sections of the southwestern part of the United States have been barren for centuries because of the lack of rain. No vegetation can grow without soil, except a few plants that receive their nourishment from the air or water, and no plant life can grow without heat and moisture.

In recent years, men have reclaimed much of these barren regions by irrigation. This process of irrigation is successful over large areas only when water from the mountains or from some source is found which is at a higher level than the area to be irrigated. Pumps have sometimes been used to raise water from a lower level to the barren area, but this is too expensive for large tracts of land, especially when the water is brought from a great distance.

The water, which falls as rain, comes from the clouds. It gets into the clouds by a process called evaporation. Water is passing into the air at all times from the earth, from the leaves of plants, from the grass, from the soil, and from the surface of bodies of water. This evaporation takes place even in very cold weather, although the process is more rapid in warm weather.

When the air is warm, it can contain more moisture than when it is cold. After the air has absorbed as much as it can hold at its temperature, it is said to be saturated. If this saturated air becomes warmer, it may then absorb more moisture, but if it becomes cooler, the clouds can no longer hold the moisture which has been absorbed and it falls as rain.

If a moisture laden cloud is carried over a high mountain by the wind, it will lose its moisture as rain by coming in contact with the cold ice and snow of the mountain top. Since this cloud has lost all of its moisture as rain in passing over this cold area, it cannot produce any rain on the other side of the mountain until it has again become saturated. This will probably cause a barren region on this opposite side of the mountain. It requires time for a cloud to absorb moisture, and, as a result, it cannot become saturated until it has traveled some distance from the mountain.

The temperature at which clouds lose their moisture is called the dew-point. A cloud may reach its dew-point by rising so high in the air as to come in contact with the cold upper atmosphere. This upper atmosphere may be so cold that the rain will freeze before it reaches the ground. Instead of falling as rain, it may fall as snow or hail.

When warm air comes in contact with any cold surface, the vapor in the warm air condenses and becomes water on the outside of the cold surface. We have learned that when a saturated cloud comes in contact with ice and snow on top of a high mountain or with the cold upper atmosphere, its vapor condenses into water and rain falls. If a glass of cold water is placed in a warm room, the vapor in the air around the glass will soon appear on the outside of the glass as water. During the night, the surface of leaves, the grass, and all vegetation become cool very much quicker than the air. The vapor of this warm air will then condense and appear on the foliage and grass as dew.

If this vapor freezes as it comes in contact with the cold grass and the foliage, it will appear as frost.

QUESTIONS

1. Why is the Sahara desert barren?

2. What conditions are necessary that vegetation may grow?

3. What are clouds? What is meant by the dew-point?

4. Why do men irrigate land? What is meant by irrigation?

5. How does rain get into the clouds?

6. What is meant by evaporation?

7. When is a cloud saturated?

8. Explain why one side of a mountain is sometimes barren.

9. Do clouds absorb moisture suddenly?

10. Where do clouds get their moisture?

11. How may a cloud lose its moisture as rain?

12. What causes snow and hail?

13. Explain why a glass "sweats."

14. What is meant by dew? What is meant by frost?

15. Do all plants need moisture for their growth?

LESSON XXXVIII

THE GOOSE

Birds or fowls may be said, in general, to be either domestic or wild. Domestic birds are those that are owned and cared for by man and, if allowed their freedom, will not leave their home. They may stray away for a considerable distance, but in the evening they will return to their roost.

Wild birds are those that do not depend on man for their food and, in general, do not stay very near to where people live.

Domestic birds do not show much fear when people approach their nest or home. Wild birds do not only attempt to conceal their home, but, in many cases, post a sentinel to give warning of the approach of a possible enemy. The chicken is a good example of a domestic bird and the crow an example of a wild bird.

The goose is found in both the wild state and as a domestic bird, although the domestic goose sometimes shows tendencies to return to the state of its wild ancestors. Among the many species of the domestic goose, the Toulouse goose and the Embden goose are the most common. The wild goose is best represented by the Canada goose on the North American continent.

The Toulouse goose in color is gray on the back and lighter on the under side. The Embden goose is white. The Canada goose is much the same in color as the Toulouse goose except that just back of the eyes there is a band of white around the head.

The goose is a very intelligent bird and may be trained to do many things. It is also very devoted to its master, almost as much so as the dog, and will protect him in case of danger. Its master must, however, treat it kindly if its devotion and loyalty are to be retained. It seems to find much pleasure in following its master around when free to do so. The goose will live to be very old if properly cared for, sometimes living to be seventy-five years old.

The most characteristic feature of the goose is its gait. It struts around as though it had something fast in its throat and were trying to get it out by stretching its neck.

The goose resembles the duck in many ways. The legs of the goose, however, are much longer than those of the duck and they seem to be placed more nearly where legs should be, being more directly under the body and not so far back. Because of this the goose can run or walk much faster than the duck, but can't swim so well as it could if its legs were placed farther back.

Geese are monogamous and mate for life. The male goose is called the gander and the little geese are called goslings. The gander will resent any attention which any other gander way show his mate and often severe battles are fought between ganders because of this attention.

The goose makes her nest in the grass or weeds near a swamp if such a location is possible. In this nest the goose lays from ten to twelve eggs. Four weeks are required to hatch these eggs. This nest is made of grass, sticks, and fine feathers plucked from the breast of the goose. The goose, in plucking these feathers from its own breast, may be compared to the rabbit in the way it makes its nest.

While the little goslings are being raised, the gander does much of the work in caring for them. While they are being taken by their parents to the creek for a swim, the gander sees to it that the little goslings do not wander away. To do this the gander generally walks behind his family and his mate leads the procession. When they return to the coop at night the gander makes certain that his family all get to their roost in safety.

The goose is an excellent swimmer. Its webbed feet are not only able to push it forward very rapidly, but also enable it to make quick turns in the water if for any reason it desires to change its course. While swimming the goose may thrust its head under the water to secure food, but it very rarely dives under the water. Its food is almost entirely vegetable in character. Grain forms a large part of its food.

Both the goose and the gander are very willing to defend themselves and their brood in case of danger. The gander seems to think that this part of the work belongs to him and cares for his brood in a very proper fashion. Their weapons of defense are their wings and their beak. With their beak they hold their victim and with their wings they strike terrific blows. Should a goose suspect that an enemy is near, it will give forth a loud squawk, and if the enemy approaches near, the goose will lower its head and advance with its mouth open and uttering a loud hissing sound something like a snake makes. This hissing seems

THE CANADA GOOSE

(Note in upper corner of picture the V-shape formation of geese in migratory flight.)

3П

to be made by the goose to express its dislike for its visitor and also to scare it away.

The domestic goose is useful for its eggs, feathers, and for meat. The feathers are plucked in the fall just before the molting season. The feathers on the breast and under the wings are the ones plucked because they are very fine in quality. These feathers are used largely for cushions, bed mattresses, and for pillows. The eggs are used for food and are about three times as large as hen eggs. They are much more highly flavored than hen eggs and are not so much in demand in the market. The flesh of the goose is not so desirable for meat as the flesh of chicken or turkey because of the great amount of fat which it contains.

Wild geese are migratory birds and spend their winters in the south, where the weather is warm. They generally go south in October and return in April. While making this flight, they arrange themselves in a definite order, generally in the shape of a V, the one at the point of the V being the leader. As they fly along high up in the sky, this leader will call to his followers and will, in turn, be answered by them by a wierd cry that is not easily forgotten when once heard. During this migration, these geese sometimes come to the earth for food and sometimes become lost in fogs and are forced to come to the earth to rest. If possible they will stop near some body of water and may take considerable corn from the nearby cornfields to use as food. In some sections of the country, farmers protect their cornfields with guns at this migratory season and thus destroy many of these geese.

The wild goose makes a nest which is very similar to that made by the domestic goose except that she lays only about five eggs in it.

Wild geese that become disabled or fatigued in their migratory flight may be domesticated if placed with domestic geese and the feathers of one wing clipped. These feathers are clipped to keep the goose from flying. At the migratory season, much care must be taken in restraining these wild geese from wandering away, so strong is their tendency to migrate at certain seasons of the year.

QUESTIONS

1. Distinguish between domestic and wild fowls.
2. To which class does the goose belong?

3. Name two kinds of domestic geese.

4. What is the most characteristic feature of the goose?

5. What is meant by the word monogamous?

6. What are young geese called?

7. What particular work in the goose family does the gander do?

8. What kind of food goes the goose eat?

9. How does the goose fight and what are its weapons of defense?

10. Of what use is the goose?

11. Why do wild geese migrate?

12. How may wild geese become domesticated?

LESSON XXXIX

THE MUSKRAT

Many of our wild animals are useful and many of them seem to serve no good purpose as far as man is concerned. Some of these, such as the woodchuck, are not only useless but destroy property and are, in reality, harmful. When we learn more about these so-called harmful wild animals, we may learn their value.

The muskrat is one of our valuable wild animals. Its fur is very useful, and in some cases its flesh is used for food.

The muskrat resembles the common rat, being brown in color, but it is very much larger. The muskrat, however, has a dark brown stripe down the middle of its back. From the tip of its nose to the end of its tail it measures from eighteen to twenty inches in length. It has small black eyes, and its ears are so small that they can scarcely be seen.

It uses the long sensitive hairs on its nose to give it information about things which it constantly touches as it moves about. The teeth of the muskrat are like those of all rodents. It has two long sharp front teeth on each jaw. Back of these front teeth is a bare space, and back of this space there are four grinders on each side.

The hind legs are much longer and stronger than the front ones. The hind feet are webbed and between the toes there are stiff tufts of hair to assist it in swimming. Its front feet are not webbed, but are equipped with sharp claws which it uses for digging.

One of the most peculiar features of the muskrat is its tail, which is covered with small scales instead of hair and is flattened very much like a knife blade. It uses its tail as a rudder when it swims.

The muskrat is covered with two coats of fur. The under coat is very thick, the hair being about one-half inch long. So fine and thick are the hairs of this under coat that it furnishes a waterproof covering for the muskrat when it goes into the water. The outer coat is very thin, the hair being one inch or more in length.

The track which the muskrat makes is different from the track made by any other animal. It will jump if it is traveling in mud or snow, its tail leaving a mark as well as its feet. If it walks along the bank of the stream in the sand its knife-like tail will leave a trail in the sand.

The muskrat lives along creeks and rivers and has two kinds of homes. If there is a considerable bank to the stream, its home will be a burrow in this bank, similar to the burrow of the woodchuck. The entrance to this burrow will be found under the surface of the water. It will always leave a small opening from its burrow to the surface of the ground to admit air. In some cases it may have an exit from its burrow to the surface of the ground, but this opening will always be well concealed by grass, logs, or drift.

If the bank of the stream is not sufficiently high for a burrow of this kind, the muskrat will make its home on the top of the ground along the bank or in a swamp, building it out of rushes, sticks, and drift. This home appears to be a pile of sticks and grass which the water often washes out on the bank of the stream. It cannot be recognized as a muskrat's home unless the observer is familiar with the muskrat and its habits.

The muskrat, like many other wild animals, has enemies. Among these enemies the most prominent are the fox, weasel, dog, and mink. Of these, the mink is the most dangerous. If any of the others pursue it, it can escape by plunging into the water. The muskrat can remain under water for several minutes and, if its home is near, it can swim under the surface until it reaches its burrow. Here it is safe from the weasel, fox, or dog. None of these animals like to go under the surface of the water. With the mink, however, it is different because the mink can go under the water just as well as the muskrat and it often follows the muskrat into its burrow and kills it. The muskrat can fight but its weapons of defense are not sufficient to cause its enemies much alarm.

The muskrat sends forth a strong scent, or odor, from two small glands located between its hind legs. This odor is not sufficiently strong nor offensive to keep its enemies from attacking it, as is true in the case of the skunk. From this odor of musk, the muskrat gets its name.

Sometimes in the spring, the water in the stream rises so high that it drowns the muskrat out of its burrow. It will then wander about homeless until it either makes another home or until the water recedes and it can use the old home. During this time when they are wandering about many are killed by dogs, foxes and other enemies.

The muskrat generally selects a place on the bank of the stream near its home where it eats its food. This place is near the edge of the water because, like the raccoon, it likes to wash its food before eating it.

During the winter months, from three to six muskrats may occupy the same home. When ice covers the surface of the water their food consists largely of roots which they can get along the bank under the ice. Its food is mainly vegetable. It will eat lilies, flags, corn, and sometimes fresh water shell fish.　During the summer when no ice is on the surface of the stream to keep them in their home, they will come and search for their food at night.

The young muskrats are born in April, June, and August.　There are generally six in each litter.　These young muskrats are well cared for by their parents until they are old enough to care for themselves.

The muskrat is of value chiefly for its fur.　This fur is taken during the cold months when the fur is best.　After the hide is dried and cured it is trimmed or shorn.　This process removes the outer coat, leaving only the thick under coat.　The hide may then be made into caps, coats, or muffs.　This fur is very often dyed when it is made into coats or other things of value.　When dyed it is offered in the market as Hudson Seal.　A muskrat hide, before it is cured, will sell in the market for about fifty cents or one dollar, and when dyed and made into coats it is of much greater value, the coats often selling for several hundred dollars.

APPLE BLOSSOMS

QUESTIONS

1. Name one difference between the woodchuck and the muskrat.

2. For what is the muskrat useful?

3. Briefly describe the appearance of the muskrat.

4. Of what value are the hairs on the nose of the muskrat?

5. Describe the teeth of the muskrat.

6. What is the difference between the hind feet and front feet of the muskrat.

7. Describe the tail of the muskrat. For what is it used?

8. What is the character of the muskrat's fur? How is it prepared for market?

9. Describe the track which the muskrat makes.

10. Where does the muskrat live and what kind of a home does it have?

11. Name the prominent enemies of the muskrat.

12. How did the muskrat get its name?

13. What and where does the muskrat eat? What other animal does the muskrat resemble in its method of eating.

14. When are the young muskrats born and how many are there in each litter?

15. How does the muskrat protect itself?

LESSON XL

THE TURTLE

The turtle is not a particular friend of the hare nor has it any special ability as a racer. It is a very humble individual and seems to be very well contented with moving along in its slow and easy fashion and interested only in attending to its own affairs.

The turtle is most peculiar in its appearance. Its head and tail look much like these of a snake. It has a beak which resembles very much the beak of the parrot. Its shell, with its hard plates and horny ridges, give us the idea that it must be afraid of meeting danger and that, to protcet itself, it carries this house-like shell around with it. The upper part of the shell is called the carapace and the under part is called the plastron.

The construction of the turtle is just as peculiar as its appearance. Instead of teeth, it has cutting knives with which it eats. It breathes through very small holes in the point of its nose which are its nostrils. It seems to swallow the air which it breathes in much the same way as a cow or horse swallows water.

Its legs are very soft and pliable but if we examine them carefully, we will find bones in them. Each of its front feet has five claws and each of its hind feet has four. In some water species, the feet are webbed for the purpose of swimming.

The turtle cannot travel rapidly because of its short legs. If it is threatened with danger by an enemy, it will force the air out through its pin-hole nostrils with a hissing sound similar to the sound made by a snake or goose. If this does not scare its enemy, it will, as a last resort, retreat inside of its shell for safety.

The food of turtles is small fish, earth worms, berries, and tender vegetation.

During the winter, they bury themselves in the mud near a stream or in the damp earth. Here they remain until the warm weather of the next spring. Turtles live to a considerable age. This age will vary with the different species, in some cases reaching the age of fifty years. Some turtles are reported to have reached the age of one hundred years. The age is sometimes indicated by dates which people sometimes carve on their shells when they find them.

In rare cases turtles are kept as pets and often become very friendly. When, however, they are compared with the dog and the goose, they are of little value as pets. The greatest value of the turtle is for food.

There are many different species of the turtle. The mud turtle lives in the water and very rarely is found on the land. The young come from eggs which the mother turtle lays in the sand on the bank of the stream. The mud turtle finds its food in the water, generally on the bottom of the stream, where it eats.

The snapping turtle is a much more vicious individual than the mud turtle and may inflict a severe injury with its sharp curved beak if one is not careful while handling it. In size it is about one foot in diameter. The soft-shelled turtle is almost the equal of the snapping turtle in viciousness.

The wood turtle is one of our most common turtles. It lives on the land and may be found in damp places, particularly in the woods. Its shell is beautifully decorated with ridges and horny plates.

The box-turtle is probably the most interesting

member of the turtle family. It is particularly well adapted for self-protection. The shell on the under side, or plastron, has a hinged door on each end. When danger threatens, it will withdraw its head, legs, and tail into its shell and then close both doors. When thus enclosed, it is very safe from most enemies.

QUESTIONS

1. Describe the appearance of the turtle.
2. Of what value is the turtle's shell?
3. How does the turtle breathe?
4. What does the turtle do when danger threatens?
5. Describe the feet of the turtle.
6. What do turtles eat?
7. Of what value are turtles?
8. To what age do turtles live?
9. Where do turtles stay in winter?
10. How is the age of turtles sometimes determined?

LESSON XLI

COLOR IN NATURE

One of the striking features of nature is color. Berries and fruit, when they are ripe, generally develop some bright color and appear in marked contrast with the foliage of the tree or vine on which they grow. The plumage of birds appears in a variety of colors. Even among animals, color is, in many cases, an important feature. What is the purpose of these colors?

There are, in general, two purposes of color in nature. One is to attract and the other is to conceal. It is evident that no particular flower, bird, animal, or other form of life can, by its color, serve both purposes at the same time.

Brilliant colors are generally for the purpose of attraction. The bright colors of flowers attract insects. When the insects come to the flower they thrust their tongue, or proboscis, down into the throat of the flower to get the nectar which the flower has stored up. During this process of securing the nectar, the insect will become dusted with the pollen grains from the stamens of the flower. These pollen grains which cling to the insect will come into contact with the pistil of the next flower from which the insect secures nectar. In this way the flowers become fertilized and seeds are produced. This process of fertilization continues as the insect goes from flower to flower. Without these visits of the insects, the flowers, in many cases, could not produce seed. The brilliant colors which attract the insects are thus of much value to the flowers.

Apples and berries also become colored when ripe for the purpose of attraction. Since all life seems to feel the responsibility of reproducing itself, the cherry becomes red to attract the birds in order that they may eat the cherries and distribute the seed. Apples become colored when ripe to attract animals. These animals eat the apples and also distribute the seed. It will be noticed that the seeds of cherries, apples, and other kinds of fruit that become colored, are not fully developed and hence not ready to be distributed or planted until the fruit has become colored or attractive. Until this time the fruit remains green in order that it may be concealed and not noticed by birds or other forms of life that may eat it. What is true of cherries and apples in this particular, is true of other kinds of fruit.

The brilliant plumage of butterflies, moths, and birds is for the purpose of either attracting their mates or for family recognition. The bright plumage of the rooster, Baltimore oriole, cardinal, and other birds is for the purpose of attracting their mates.

Many forms of life develop color for the purpose of protection. The rabbit is brown like the leaves in which it hides. The toad has the same color as the ground over which it travels and in which it passes the winter. The katydid is green like the leaves of the tree on which it is found. The grasshopper, when flying, is easily seen but when it alights in the grass or weeds, it seems to have disappeared completely so closely does it resemble its surroundings in color. The female bird, in most cases, has a plumage which is very dull in color in order that she may not be easily seen while she is sitting on her nest and hatching her eggs. The tiger is striped to resemble the trees of the jungle in which it hides. These stripes always extend in a vertical direction so that they may blend with the trunks of trees and shrubs.

The monarch butterfly, although it has a very bright color, does not seem to be afraid of its enemies, which are mostly birds, because it is very distasteful to any bird that may attempt to eat it. The birds seem to have discovered this and do not molest it. The viceroy butterfly does not have either an odor or taste which is unpleasant to birds and, in order to protect itself, it has developed almost the same color and markings of the monarch butterfly. This is true not only of these butterflies, but it is also true of their larvae. This marked resemblance in color gives the viceroy the same protection as the monarch has from any injury from birds.

The under or ventral side of fish is light in color that they may not easily be seen by their enemies from below. The dorsal or upper side is dark in color in order that they may blend in color with the bed of the stream when seen by enemies from above.

Many forms of life change their color when their surroundings are changed, or when they are placed in an environment which is unnatural to them. A toad, if placed in a white porcelain tub, will become much lighter in color in a very few days. The ptarmigan is chestnut colored on the head and neck and marked with black, the back and rump are black with bars of yellowish-brown and these colors protect it in the summer. In winter it changes its color to white. As it spends its winters in the snow-clad regions its white plumage conceals it. Some of our fur-bearing animals of the north are white in winter when the snow covers the ground and become much darker in color when the snow disappears. This change of color is largely for the purpose of concealment or for the purpose of making them less conspicuous in their surroundings.

The men who had charge of affairs in the world war made use of this principle of protective coloring. Ships were painted in such a way that they resembled the waves or sky and, because of this coloring were not easily seen by enemies. Machine gun locations were covered with brush and even, in some cases, the guns themselves were so painted that they resembled their surroundings. Even the uniforms of the soldiers were of such a color that they might resemble the color of the forest or shrubbery in which they might be hiding. The change in the uniforms of the American soldiers from blue to brown was largely due to an accurate observation of how nature protects her different forms of life from their enemies.

QUESTIONS

1. For what two purposes does color exist in nature?

2. What are the two kinds of color found in nature?

3. For what does each kind of color exist?

4. Name one purpose of the color found in flowers.

5. How does this color in flowers serve its purpose?

6. Why do apples and berries become colored? When does this color appear?

7. What is the appearance of apples and berries before they change color?

8. What purpose does the first color of fruit serve?

9. What is the purpose of color in butterflies, moths, and birds?

10. Why is the rabbit brown in color?

11. Name three other kinds of life and give reasons for their particular color.

12. Why is the viceroy butterfly so colored?

13. Give a reason for the color of fish.

14. Why do some forms of life change their colors?

15. In what way was color used in the world war?

WILD CARROT—QUEEN ANNE'S LACE

IN THE OPEN AIR
BY
GEORGE W. DORLAND
Principal, New York City Schools.

This book was written to arouse the interest of boys and girls in various aspects and phases of Nature, more or less generally observable through the school year. Children over ten years of age who possess average reading ability should be able to assimilate the material with a minimum of assistance.

Boys and girls reared in the commercial environment of our larger towns and cities need at least an occasional reminder that there are other things in life than buying and selling, and the making of money. Even children who are fortunate enough to reside in suburban or rural districts all too often look upon the world about them with unseeing eyes and a lack of appreciation of many of its really important happenings.

Many prose and poetical excerpts from well-known authors have been introduced, to induce the readers' further interest in what poets and others have thought and felt about Nature.

NATURE STUDY
FOR BOYS AND GIRLS
WITH A
MANUAL OF INSTRUCTION

by John Bradford Craig, Pittsburgh Schools, Pittsburgh, Pennsylvania. Endorsed by Superintendents and Nature Study Instructors as suitable for grade work.

A series of textbooks for the grades. Fully illustrated with halftones, zinc etchings and pictures in natural colors. Covers all of the work from the third grade to the sixth grade.

"It is well graded, and the story is told in a language that can be understood by boys and girls. It avoids confusion of fiction and fact and will hold the interest of the pupil by the simple statement of facts."

The stories and facts presented not only develop interest on the part of the pupil, but give him a setting and a perspective for his observation. The pupil gets the utilitarian and ethical sides of nature brought close to him while he is interested.

These books are intended to help the pupil get acquainted with his neighbors. He ought to have this chance. **These neighbors can render him a great service if he knows them.** He must know them first before they can serve him.

It has the virtue of not being scientific for science's sake, and in my judgment it will be well accepted by the progressive school systems of the country.—William M. Davidson, Superintendent of Schools, Pittsburgh, Pennsylvania.

McINDOO PUBLISHING COMPANY
Kansas City, Missouri